IN PRAISE OF

POETRY

OLGA SEDAKOVA

POETRY

IN PRAISE OF

Translated from the Russian and Edited by
Caroline Clark, Ksenia Golubovich & Stephanie Sandler

OPEN LETTER
LITERARY TRANSLATIONS FROM THE UNIVERSITY OF ROCHESTER

First edition, 2014
All rights reserved

Library of Congress Cataloging-in-Publication Data: Available upon request.
ISBN-13: 978-1-940953-02-1 / ISBN-10: 1-940953-02-2

This project is supported in part by an award from the National Endowment for the Arts.

ART WORKS.
arts.gov

*This publication was made possible with the support of the Mikhail Prokhorov Foundation
TRANSCRIPT Programme to Support Translations of Russian Literature.*

Printed on acid-free paper in the United States of America.

Text set in Jenson Pro, an old-style serif typeface drawn by Robert Slimbach,
based on a Venetian old-style text face cut by Nicolas Jenson in 1470.

Design by N. J. Furl

Open Letter is the University of Rochester's nonprofit, literary translation press:
Lattimore Hall 411, Box 270082, Rochester, NY 14627

www.openletterbooks.org

CONTENTS

IN PRAISE OF POETRY

INTRODUCTION

by Stephanie Sandler

Olga Sedakova stands out among contemporary Russian poets as a poet blessed with the talents of musicality, verbal agility, and insights into the workings of soul and mind. An erudite writer who wears her knowledge lightly, she deftly draws other poetic traditions into her work, balancing openness to European and American cultural traditions with a profound knowledge of Russian cultural and religious traditions. In presenting a new translation of her work into English, our book aims to show Sedakova as a Russian poet and as a creator of world poetry.

We offer here two poetic cycles: one based on Slavic folk traditions ("Old Songs," her shimmering sequence that mixes folk and biblical wisdom), and one that emerges from European myths ("Tristan and Isolde," perhaps her most mysterious long poem). Sedakova's capacious account in prose of her own poetic development ("In Praise of Poetry") follows. Alongside these three major texts, we have included our interview with the poet conducted in 2012 and, as a coda, the poetic credo she presented when she was presented with The Masters Translation Prize in Moscow in 2011, awarded by the Masters of Literary Translation Guild. All of these texts appear in English in full for the first time.

BECOMING A POET

Olga Sedakova was born in Moscow in 1949 into an educated family;
her father was an engineer, and her sister Irina is a highly regarded
linguist. She studied at the Philological Faculty of Moscow State
University and the Institute of Slavic and Balkan Studies, where she
completed a graduate degree in 1983 in ethnography and ancient
studies with a dissertation on ancient Slavic funeral rituals (pub-
lished in 2004). Sedakova learned multiple European languages, and
she worked for nearly a decade as a reader of foreign scholarship for
a major Moscow library, INION. At a relatively early moment in her
training as a scholar, her teachers agreed that her destiny was to be a
poet. But this poetry did not appear in mainstream publications save
for a very few poems she wrote as a young girl. A Russian-language
volume was published in Paris in 1986, and her work soon began to
reach an audience within Russia beyond the underground circles of
intellectuals and poets in Moscow, Leningrad, and Tartu. The first
substantial publication of her poetry in Russia was in 1988, during
Glasnost. These poems were a stunning departure from the mostly
politicized, even sensational work of the late 1980s. They seemed
an uncanny reminder of deeply dormant spiritual traditions and a
joyous re-imagining of formal, rhythmic, and lexical possibilities in
the Russian language.

It would have been impossible to know, in 1988, how the public
stature of Sedakova would, by the start of the twenty-first century,
match up to her formidable gifts. It is fair to say that her reputation
has risen to make her first among equals. Sedakova's achievements
have now been recognized in Europe and in Russia by many awards:
the 1983 Andrei Bely Prize; Paris Prize for a Russian Poet, 1991;
the Alfred Toepfer Pushkin Prize, awarded in Hamburg, 1994; the
European Poetry Prize, Rome, 1995; the Solovyov Literary Prize,

awarded in the Vatican, 1998; the Solzhenitsyn Literary Prize, Moscow, 2003; the Chevalier d'honneur d'Ordre des Arts et des Lettres de la République Française, 2005 (and Officer status in 2012); the Dante Alighieri Prize, 2011, awarded in Italy; and many more besides. This kind of recognition has been made possible by her ability to reach readers in multiple languages. Excellent translations of her work now exist in Italian, French, Hebrew, Ukrainian, German, Albanian, and Danish. Most important, the work has now appeared in Russian in Russia, and extensively so. A handsome two-volume set of her poetry and prose appeared in 2001, and in 2010 a four-volume edition was published, including the full range of her essays on philology, philosophy, theology, cultural and literary studies, as well as her translations from nearly a dozen languages. Along the way, individual volumes offered collections of her poetry, her travel writings, her philosophical-political essays, and even two books of children's poetry. A signal achievement was the publication in 2005 of her dictionary of "difficult words"—words whose meanings had changed across the centuries, words still in use in contemporary Russian but with meanings different from that of the Slavic Orthodox ritual and in the biblical tradition. Sedakova had long collected these words, and published the dictionary so that people could understand what it was they were saying in church (she has been told by grateful priests that for the first time they understood prayers they had chanted for decades; the dictionary is now in its third edition). Such is this poet's knowledge of the Russian language, and of its many layers.

In her own poetry, Sedakova's facility in using the many meanings of words became the foundation on which her creative work as preserver of ancient meanings and seer into the new would be placed. Is there another poet in any language who is as perfectly balanced between profound knowledge of the poetic, philosophical, and theological tradition and fearless invention of a new word? The repeated image in her poems of an entity balanced on a needle's tip conveys this sense of precarious bodily awareness, and we often feel ourselves teetering between worlds when reading her work.

How does one become such a poet? The essay "In Praise of Poetry" is Sedakova's own answer to that question. It is a tale of education and self-education, an account of a child's wonder and horror at the world, all blended with a meditation on the nature of the poetic word and of the psyche in which that word comes into being. Olga Sedakova had many educations, as she tells the tale. Alongside her training in literature and philology, there was an ever-growing knowledge of church ritual and religious history, learned from her grandmother, her priests (her *dukhovnye ottsy*), and her friends, some of whom have been remarkable thinkers and philosophers (like V. V. Bibikhin, Sergei Averintsev, and Yuri Lotman, all now deceased). Along the way, she learned many languages, both ancient (Latin, Greek, Old Church Slavonic) and modern (French, German, English, and her beloved Italian). She became a gifted, experienced translator, rendering works by Dante, Petrarch, Dickinson, Pound, Eliot, Claudel, Mallarmé, Rilke, Celan, and others into remarkable Russian poems. Sedakova's prose, of which she has written more in the last decades, includes studies of such modern poets as Pushkin, Pasternak, Zabolotsky, and Khlebnikov, as well as memoirs and memorials to contemporaries she honors—Venedikt Erofeev, Viktor Krivulin, and Sergei Averintsev among them.

A number of her essays have treated matters of religion, doctrine, theology, and ethics, and those essays boldly name the real dangers of "moralia" and firmly strike a balance among several risks. As one sees in many passages in "Praise," Sedakova is not one to embrace dogma or to strike a moralistic tone, but she is also not ready to relinquish the belief that words have ethical force in the world, nor to give up on the hope that the poetic word may yet have particular, special insight to offer. Moralistic thinking, she argues, pushes people to diminish the value of imagination and aesthetics. Sedakova might well agree with the strong statement of American poet and thinker Allen Grossman, that poetry is a means by which "human beings engage, as they can, in the maintenance of a human world in which they can meet one another, affirm one another, remember, see, and foresee one another."[1] Affirming our humanity is one of the gifts of poetry, and in Sedakova's terms that means a refusal of the world's many pressures toward mediocrity. Poetry, she tells us, is a radical expression of knowledge about another way of life. What is most radical is the form, which can be a containment of explosive force. Sedakova's own work abounds in this kind of formal transformation, with astonishing beauty in her "Old Songs" and in "Tristan and Isolde," which is in some ways about the very idea of transformation.

"OLD SONGS"

Among Sedakova's cycles of short poems, "Old Songs" stands out for its astonishing and completely deceptive simplicity. It is her finest demonstration of a view that she articulates in "Praise": that "poetry is a gift, a gift blessed by heaven and earth." The poems are a form of praise for life on the blessed earth. Although there are actual moments of prayer, for the most part "Old Songs" feels closer to the dailiness of the monastic chroniclers than to the intensity of words addressed toward God or of pious sermons. Events of domestic life are interwoven with intimations of the larger cosmic orders. When there is wisdom, it is that of the people, the *narod*. When there is advice, it is enigmatic, even gnomic. The lexicon is biblical at times, even occasionally elevated, but there are no specialized words, no obscure theological turns of phrase. It is all astonishingly concrete, built from the simplest of words—stone, child, servant, word, horse, dog, fish, cradle, spruce, garden, star. The elements that fill out the life of the world are gently rearranged, poem after poem, with steadying, organizing pressure exerted from words that designate larger forces. They might be saints' names, or biblical names, or references to angels or even to God. The result is a sure sense of the order of the universe, its harmonious and capacious embrace of all that is righteous and errant, all that is life and life after death. The voice who gently asks for a walking stick to go out into the garden makes nothing of the fact that it speaks from the grave; the lullaby reassures the baby that dreams of becoming an ocean wave or an angel of the Lord are equally within reach.

"Old Songs" comprises three notebooks, the very name of which gives them the feel of found manuscripts; one wonders whether Sedakova, who has translated and much admires Emily Dickinson, might not have had in mind her habit of sewing pages of poems together in fascicles. Something of Dickinson's world in fact is felt in these poems, all short and poised between the worlds of nature and spirit. But whereas Dickinson's poems most often rely on the common meter of hymns, Sedakova writes her "Old Songs" without the shaping structures of regular meters (save in one poem, the exceptional "Marching Song"), although she does use occasional rhyme and a great deal of lexical repetition and other syntactic patterning, so much so that the usage of free verse becomes not so much an occasion for liberation from traditional meters as the shaping envelope in which intricate patterning can roam freely. As the poet Mikhail Gronas has noted, "Old Songs" is one of the most successful long cycles of contemporary Russian poetry to rely on free verse, in part because of the contrast created by the form with the emphatically traditional content.[2] And it is indeed a long cycle, the poet's longest, totaling thirty-nine poems. A sense of careful placement of poems creates moments of counterpoint and lovely echoes of words, images, and stanzaic patterns. Each publication of the cycle, and there have been several since its first complete appearance in 1990, has printed one poem per page, allowing a generous frame of blank white page to offer itself to the reader for beholding and contemplation. Our translation preserves that sense of silent pause between poems.

"TRISTAN AND ISOLDE"

If "Old Songs" presents complex ideas beneath a surface of seeming simplicity, then "Tristan and Isolde," a cycle of twelve poems and three preludes from 1978-82, may at first appear to be something of the opposite. We are in the presence of a complex, high-culture text, one with multiple allusions and perhaps many sources. Some readers may think immediately of Wagner's opera, although Sedakova's indirect account of Tristan and Isolde's romance will feel quite unlike the opera; medieval romance versions, as retold by Gottfried von Strassbourg and Sir Thomas Malory, are more pertinent. When we are bid to listen in the poem's first prelude, we are addressed very much in the mode of Gottfried's romance, but Sedakova's poem cycle does not recount the story of Tristan and Isolde's love. It promises a tale of "love and death," but the plot elements most associated with the tale of Tristan and Isolde—drinking a love potion meant for someone else, voyage by ship, escape to the forest, punishment among the lepers, and the love triangle itself—are barely mentioned. "Tristan and Isolde" is mysterious at its core, inviting readers to discover slowly what it has to say about the tale of the two famous lovers. One begins to suspect, on reading the cycle's preludes and its many small diversions, that Sedakova means to keep the myth at some distance, to use its motifs sparsely, chiefly as an impetus to meditate on the

11

enduring fates of illness and betrayal, of journeys and divination, of death and immortality. Yet she also presents as well a searching exploration of the myth—its music, its symbols, its profoundly tragic understanding of love's travails. An ethos of Christian sacrifice and journey toward salvation seems as significant in the poem as any quest for love's redemption, and in her account of Tristan and Isolde, we see how the renunciations of love are as powerfully felt as its pleasures. Unlike the myth of Lancelot and Guinevere, with its central quest for the Holy Grail, the tale of Tristan and Isolde has only to do with love, with impossible, all-consuming love.

The re-telling of a myth is a potentially conservative, even staid art form, but Sedakova's "Tristan and Isolde" attains a kind of wildness that belies any such notion. Some of that wildness is a matter of tone, as when the speaker asks rhetorically how she could possibly know where exactly the waves will travel, or how far the eye can see. The poem calls into question the narrative truths of the myth, and they suggest an allegory that motivates the poem's refusal to tell stories forthrightly: as the people to whom poets speak are now diminished and poor, so must be the story they are told, even if it comes from a tradition that is ennobled and honored. The word "poor" (*bednyi*) is heard often in Sedakova's poetry, and it means something different from the modernists' frequent complaint of exhausted narratives. Sedakova's notion of poverty is linguistic, a kind of stripped-down lexicon where decorative or diverting words have been banished, where a narrowed verbal range creates new reverberations and greater ambiguities. The restricted vocabulary paradoxically enriches the poem's music.

Formally, "Tristan and Isolde" offers another sort of intrigue. The poems are metrically varied. One of the poems is trochaic, but most are iambic, with varying line lengths and with a number of lines that have extra beats. Several poems feature many short lines mixed in, and most of the poems use rhyme. The effect of these formal choices is just slightly unsettling, inducing a kind of rough texture or rippling, changing unevenness. To hear the poet read the poem, which one can do on several currently available recordings, is also to hear the gentle presence of regular rhythms.[3]

Listening is in fact one of the poem's supreme pleasures. At the poem's first lines, when listeners are gathered around to listen, the invitation comes with a beckoning to join in sewing a "dress of darkness." Coming into the world of Tristan and Isolde, we in a sense close our eyes. This is one of Sedakova's supreme metaphors for the advent of the imagination—it has led her to write movingly of the images of blindness in Rembrandt, for example, and of a childhood memory that associated impending blindness with the fantasy of a completely different universe.[4] If the pictures are often suffused with darkness that is partly an aesthetic choice—Sedakova herself would later ask that we think about why Rembrandt's paintings grow so dark—and it is also a kind of cognitive pre-condition, a way of urging us to close our eyes to the daily sights of life in order to focus the mind more completely on the vision of a dwarf telling fortunes from the stars, or on two unnamed lovers who lie entwined in the darkness, guarded by their faithful dog. Sedakova's poem is, among its many other virtues, an act of instruction, an imperative that we see and hear the elements of a living myth.

"IN PRAISE OF POETRY"

Sedakova's essay about her growth as a poet, rather than speaking in a gesture of command, itself seems to respond to a command. The essay opens as if spoken to a knowing friend, Vladimir Saitanov, who asked that she write down the origins for her early work. Sedakova creates a conversational and easy tone, even when complex matters are broached. She refers to poems, historical events, or cultural landmarks without pausing for explanation (our translation includes many notes to aid readers necessarily further from the cultural context). "In Praise of Poetry" looks back to the years of childhood and adolescence. Sedakova later explained that this essay allowed her to combine two genres: the tale of childhood, for her epitomized by Tolstoy's *Childhood*, and that of *ars poetica*. She wanted to communicate the happiness of her own childhood, and to offer "musings on the nature of poetry."[5]

In the early recollections of poetry, Sedakova presents both her gently skeptical, adult view of her youthful enthusiasms and also a certain steady regard for the purity of those early feelings. The essay includes some of her earliest efforts as a poet. She neither sentimentalizes childhood nor shows a child's moments of incomprehension as silly; in fact she singles out three poets—Khlebnikov, Pasternak, and Rilke—for showing us both the world and language as if with a child's inability to render any impressions as automatic, but also without any sense of amazement. Sedakova perceives a splendid paradox in such poetry, which can be difficult for readers to grasp precisely because of its simplicity. Simplicity itself is no simple concept in Sedakova's work, as she shows in describing the speech of her grandmother: it is a language made up of names, not words; it has an unconscious originality, the "originality of the pre-verbal world itself." This language may seem unsophisticated, exuding no erudition, but its ability to match objects or ideas to words is nearly fathomless. These traits mark "Old Songs" as well, a text linked to "In Praise of Poetry" by the figure of the grandmother, as muse and as addressee.

A powerful presence in the essay is the world of music. Sedakova was lucky enough to have a music teacher who also introduced her to poetry, including the work of Rilke. Her music teacher, Mikhail Erokhin, had a wonderful way of inviting her to imagine entire spaces in which pieces of music resounded. A Bach prelude, for example, was presented to her as an evolving, brief narrative: "An old man enters his empty quarters and lights a candle, a corridor lit up behind him unfolds its dimensions; before him is a darkness which can only be sensed, invisible and unfathomable to the eye." Music may be the supremely important art form for this poet, both for its example of melody, harmony, precision, rhythmic balancing, and for its status among forms of aesthetic expression—its potential purity and distance from burdensome semantic elaboration, its association with divinity and the sublime. Music flourishes as a metaphor in Sedakova's work. "Old Songs" invokes music in the cycle's title and in the use of lyrical form. "Tristan and Isolde" can be understood as a kind of musically structured work in its own right. "In Praise of Poetry" abounds in references to musical works in addition to its fine account of the poet's own musical training. It often uses musical terms to describe poetic phenomena, as when the poet says that she knows only one way of composing a poem, toward a crescendo. The essay itself concludes on a high note: poetry, Sedakova tells us, may "give a voice to that which is silent." She means here something as much spiritual as ethical. Her praise in this essay is for the "sacred and utterly audacious act of humility performed by poetry."

Our book concludes with an interview with the poet, conducted in December, 2012, and including specific questions about the texts translated here. Readers may thus hear the poet reflecting on these texts from a later vantage point. As we were preparing the interview and polishing our translations, Olga Sedakova was awarded a translation prize in Moscow. Her acceptance speech seemed the perfect way for us to end this book, allowing the poet to articulate for us the standard we hoped to achieve in translating her work.

We take the occasion of this publication to thank the poet for permission to translate her work, and for her participation in our translation process. We are grateful to her for answering questions, looking at drafts, and providing much information that has informed the notes to "In Praise of Poetry." Readers will sense that some notes are in fact written by her. Francesca Chessa, Italian translator of "In Praise of Poetry" has been especially helpful to us as well. Warm thanks to all.

OLD SONGS

(Translated by Stephanie Sandler)

FIRST NOTEBOOK

What glitters white on the greening slope?
- A. S. Pushkin

1. OFFENSE

What are you doing, spiteful offense?
I fall asleep, but you do not,
I awaken, and you are already up,
staring at me, like a fortune-teller.

Can you say who offended me?
No, not one—only God, all-powerful.
He permits offense to some,
but holds it back from others.

Or maybe life failed to love me?
No, untrue, life feels pity and love,
it keeps me safe in a secret place
and will fetch me when it wants
to look at me with a matchless gaze.

What are you doing, spiteful offense,
Sitting before me, like a fortune-teller?

Will you say that I live badly, that
I offend the sickly and the sufferers?

2. THE STEED

A traveler rides along a dark road,
he rides without hurrying, rides on and on.

"Ask me, my steed, whatever you like,
ask me anything—I will answer it all.
People will not listen to my words,
and God knows all without my tales.

How very strange it all is:
Why does fire burn in this world,
why do we fear midnight,
does anyone feel happiness?

I will say—but you will not believe—
how much I love the nighttime road,
how much I love this banishment
and tomorrow they will banish me again.

So come nearer, time of mercy, of healing,
drink down the hangovers of my youth,
draw forth the stinger of young years
from the fresh hot wound—
and then I shall be the wisest of all!"

The steed does not speak, but an answer is heard,
the long road draws onward.
And no one on this earth is happy.
And the unhappy? They are remarkably few.

3. FORETOLD FATE

Who can possibly know what fate will hold?
He who divines the future fails to see fate.

Perhaps even you may someday remember me,
while I shall forget you completely.

I shall appear then silently,
as the unliving come quietly to the living,
and I shall say that I know something
that you will never learn.

And then I will kiss your hand,
as servants kiss their masters.

4. CHILDHOOD

I remember early childhood,
and a dream in a bed of gold.

A dream? Or perhaps truth:
someone sees me, someone
comes in quickly from the garden
and stands there, smiling.

"The world," he says, "is a desert.
The human heart—a stone.
People love what they do not know.

Don't forget me, Olga,
and I will forget no one."

5. SIN

You can deceive the high heavens—
for high heaven cannot possibly see everything.
You can deceive deepest earth—
for deep earth sleeps, and hears nothing.
Clairvoyants, fortune-tellers, and seers are fair game—
but you will never deceive your own self.

Alas, mirrors, glass panes, and forest streams
love not the sinner among us:
strangers' blood courses there like the wind,
and twists like a serpent in pain.

"Tomorrow we shall awaken early
and go to see the fortune-teller,
we shall give her money for her work
so she may tell us—
she sees nothing. Nothing."

6.

There is a mean and spiteful man,
an unkind man, a sufferer.
Oddly, I feel sorry for him,
but I am even more unkind.

And once when we were talking,
too long ago to remember when,
it was nighttime, with endless rain,
as if it had fallen deep into thought,
as if someone had stepped down
to walk all in tears, as if made of tears:

not about self, not about sky,
not about winding stairs,
not about all that is past,
not about all that will be—

nothing will be.
Nothing can be.

7. CONSOLATION

Do not try to guess about your own death
and do not smile, when all is lost,
do not think of how they will mourn you,
how their regret, too late, will sting them.

This is a poor consolation, and
an amusement that offends the earth.

Better you should speak and think to yourself:
what glitters white on the greening slope?

On the green slope the orchards play
and go down to the water's edge,
like little lambs with golden bells.
White lambs on the greening slope.

But death will come, asking no one.

8. THE ARGUMENT

Have I not lived on this earth a long time?
Adding it up, out loud, is enough to cause fear.
Yet even now the heart loves not itself.
It paces, a prisoner in its cell—
but what it doesn't see in that window!

Then an old woman had this to say:
"How good, how warm to be in God's world.
Like peas in a pod, we lie in rows,
we lie in the hands of the Lord.
The one you seek—will not return.
Anything you ask—will not be done.
Even this will gladden the heart,
like sweet-tasting grains
offered to a bird in its ornate cage—
this gift, too, is not in vain."

I nodded, but said under my breath:
enough, you foolish old woman.
Anything is possible, and then some.

9. SUPPLICATION

What poor, miserable people!
They are not evil, just impatient:
they eat bread—and hunger for more,
they drink—and the wine sobers them.

If asked,
I should say: O God,
make of me something new!

I love the greatness of miracle
and have no love for misfortune.

Make of me a stone, all faceted,
and then lose it, dropped from the ring finger
onto desert sands.

Let it lie quietly,
not inside, not outside,
but everywhere, as a mystery.

And no one would see it,
Only the light inside and the light outside.

And the light is like children at play,
like small children, and tamed beasts.

10. THE WORD

He who loves will be loved in return.
He who serves shall be served—
if not now, then another time, later.

But the best reward comes of gratitude,
he shall walk forth, his work finished, and without Rachel
feel happy, climbing green hills.

You, word, are the robes of Kings,
a dress of patience, both long and short,
more lofty than the sky, more joyous than the sun.

Our eyes will not see
your color—a color near to us, and dear,
no human ears shall hear the noise
of your swishing, broad pleats,

only the heart will say to itself:
"You are free, and you shall be free,
and you shall not answer to slaves."

SECOND NOTEBOOK

Dedicated to my grandmother

1. BRAVERY AND MERCY

The sun shines upon just and unjust alike,
and the earth is nowhere the worse:
you can go west or east,
or wherever you are told,
you can simply stay at home.

Bravery steers the ships
on the wide oceans.
Mercy rocks the cradle of reason,
a cradle deep as it is decrepit.

He who knows bravery, knows also mercy,
for they are as sisters:
bravery is the easiest thing in the world,
the easiest of all deeds—is charity.

2. MARCHING SONG

To France there journeyed two grenadiers, escaped from confinement
    in Russia,
Their jackets were covered completely in dust, and France was also
    all dusty.

How strange it now seems. Life suddenly settles, like ashes,
Like snow on the roads of Smolensk, or sand on the steppes of
    Arabia.

And vision goes further, and further, the sky most visible of all.
"What dost Thou want, o Lord, what dost Thou want from Thy
    slave?"

Above our every desire, a lash of sorts rests, waiting to be seen.
Would that my eyes had not seen. But it is ordained that they see.

And so they shall see. Is anything impossible above this humble and
    vulgar earth?
How high does the fateful comet's fire play with light, before it
    blazes forth?

Arise, then, stand forth, o wretched comrade! Soldiers should not
    laze about.
We drink to the faith that lives unto death: beyond that, disloyalty
    has no abode.

3. THE UNFAITHFUL WIFE

Since the day you came home
and did not look at me,
everything changed inside.

Like that sick dog who
lies there sighing,
so does my soul languish and pine.

For the sinner, the whole world intercedes,
but for the innocent, only a miracle.
So let there be a miracle as witness unto me.

Show Your truth, o God,
show him that I am truthful!

Suddenly the dog, that poor creature,
shook his head quickly,
ran up to her happily,
licked her hand tenderly—
and fell down to the earth, dead.

God knows things about a man
that he himself does not know.

4. ASSURANCE

Even if they shall laugh at you and make fun,
you shall lie there as Lazarus did,
lie still and silent before the heavens—
even then shall you not be as Lazarus.

Alas, it is good to be likened
unto the black earth from the garden,
to the many-colored dust from the road,

to the cry of the smallest child, forgotten,
left behind in the fields . . .

no other thing do they ask of you.

5. LULLABY

On a hill, in a rare forest of spruce,
on the highest, delicate treetop,
a cradle is fastened.

The wind rocks it.

There with the cradle is a little cage,
and with the cage, a hollow spruce tree.

In the cage, a clever bird sings
and burns, as brightly as a candle.

Sleep, it says, sleep my little dove,
when you awake, your dreams will come true:
you can be poor, you can be rich,
you can be a wave on the ocean sea,
you can be an angel of the Lord.

6. THE RETURN: A POEM ABOUT ALEKSEI

How goodly it is to simply return:
to a city, where all is changed,
to a garden, where some trees
are distant stumps, others
creak in the wind, as they never did before,
or to a house, where they grieve that you're gone.

To return, and not to say one's name.
To be silent, then, unto death.

Let them guess for themselves,
let them ask passersby,
let them understand, and yet understand it not.

And the objects of the world shine,
like tiny distant stars.

7. DESIRE

There's no telling what's occurred to me:
when someone, anyone, is praised,
then I should be praised still more,
but for what?—that's not for me to say;

or, that there is no such anger,
no endlessly forgotten village,
and no creature so worthless,
that a spirit could not rise overhead,
a wondrous fife singing out to its treasure;

that there is no death among deaths
whose forces could be set against
my patient, slow-moving life,
like wormwood and weeds—

There's no telling what's occurred to me
and will occur, year after year.

8. THE MIRROR

My dearest one, even I do not know
Why such things exist:

a mirror hovers nearby
no bigger than a lentil
or a grain of millet.

But what burns and flickers within it,
what looks out, flares, and fades—
better not to see that at all.

Life, after all—is a not a very large thing:
all of it, every bit, can gather itself up
on the tip of a finger, the end of an eyelash.
And death spreads all around it, a vast sea.

9. THE VISION

I look out at you, but it is not you I see:
my old father in another's clothes.
As if he cannot take a step,
even as they chase him, chase him.

O God, I think, o my God,
maybe I am soon to die—
and so I feel pity all around?

For the beasts, because they are beasts,
and water, because it flows,
and the wicked man, because of his misfortune,
and myself, because I have gone out of my mind.

10. THE HOUSE

We shall live for a long time, as long
as trees live next to the water,
as water washes over their roots,
and earth opens out toward the sky,
as Elizabeth goes out to meet Mary.

We shall live for a long, long time.
We shall build two tall houses:
one made of gold, one of darkness,
and both making the sounds of the sea.

They shall think that we are already gone . . .
Right then and there, we shall tell them:

"The heart of a person floats off
on water that is unseen, swift.
There, do you see it? Old time flies past,
like the dove from the days of Noah."

11. THE DREAM

The Prodigal Son is having a dream,
Lying on his deathbed, he dreams
he is leaving home.

He wears cheerful garments,
and his great-grandfather's ring.
His brother leads out his horse.

Early in the morning, it can be so fine:
the blast of horns and strings from the rear,
ahead, the playing is better still.

And the dogs, the servants, their wives,
have gathered at the gates to watch,
they are wishing him safe passage.

12. THE CONCLUSION

In every unhappy thing
there hides a ring or a secret note
left, as agreed, in a tree hollow.

In every word there is a road,
a melancholy and passionate path.

And the one who said yes, who is ready,
his tears flow, but not for this,
his hopes will be utterly different.

The one who knows no hope—shall have none.
The one who knows—shall again feel wonder,
shall smile openly in the mind,
and praise the mercy of God.

1981

POEMS WITH NO PLACE
IN THE SECOND NOTEBOOK

THE FEAST

If he reads the stars,
or lays out stones, like cards,
and boils up sand and needles
to learn what comes
out of all that now is—
even so, he will discover very little.

Life—is a young wine.
No matter how much you drink,
it will not dull your mind
or loosen your tongue.
Better not even to start.

But when the candles are snuffed out
and everyone leaves to go home
or nods off at the table—
then it's frightening to think
from whom you sought counsel,
and what matters you discussed,
where you have been, and why.

ANOTHER LULLABY

Sleep, my little dove, no one shall leave you,
leave you to be looked at by others,
as the woman gone out to harvest
left her son at the edge of the field.
She reaps the barley and wipes away tears.

"Mama, mama, who walks toward me,
who stands towering above me?"

Three old women with powers of magic,
or—three old she-wolves, all gone gray.
They rock your cradle, they coo you to sleep,
they chew the poppy seeds into softness.
But the child has no need of poppy seeds.
The child cries, but no one hears.

OLD WOMEN

As patient as an old artist,
I love to look long and hard
at the faces of devout and spiteful old women:
their mortal lips
and the immortal strength
that has pressed their lips together.

(It's as if an angel sits there,
stacking money into columns:
five-kopeck pieces and lesser ones . . .
Shoo!—he says to the children,
birds, and beggars—
shoo, he says, go away:
can't you see that I'm busy?)

I look—and I draw a picture in my mind:
myself before a dark mirror.

BEADS

My grandmother's lapis ring,
my great grandfather's books—these
I can give up, I think.
But somehow these glass beads
are more than I can bear to lose.

They are bright-colored, simple
like a garden of peacocks, and
their heart is made of stars and fish scales.

Or a lake, and fish in the lake:
first a black one dives up, then scarlet,
then the tiniest fish, a flash of green—
he will never come back now,
indeed, why should he?

I love not the poor, nor the rich,
not this country, nor any other,
not the time of day, nor time of year—
but I do love what is all-seeming:
it is a mysterious form of joy.
It has no price—and no sense.

THE JOURNEY

When this misfortune comes to an end
or this happiness turns away,
it will move off like the towering waves,

and I will walk down a familiar road,
at last, going where I am bidden to go.

Then I shall listen to what I will hear,
Speak, that I may hear these words:

"I have been waiting for you—and here you are.
I have always known you and now recognize you.
Can you think I would forget?"

Each of us wants to be recognized, known,
for birds to fly down in greeting,
for the dead to stand up as if living,
for the beasts to bring their young

and for time, slowly, to unfold,
like lightning remembered from long ago.

THE THIRD NOTEBOOK

In memory of my grandmother,
Darya Semyonovna Sedakova

1

Come, joy of my life, let us go,
let's walk around our garden,
and look at what has changed in the world!

Give me your hand, my sweet, my love,
bring me my old walking stick.
Let's go, before summer passes by.

No matter that I lie in my grave—
there's no end to what one forgets!
From the garden, you can see a small river,
in the river, you see every last fish.

2

Now what have I done, that
my candle cannot flame brightly,
that it flickers like eyes in pain,
like sleepless, dull eyes?—

I will remember—much; I shall forget—even more.
But I do not want to forget, nor to remember.

Ah, I have looked long on people in this world
and I know strange things:
I know that the soul is but a babe,
a babe until its last hour of life,

it believes everything—everything!
and it sleeps in a den of thieves.

3

A woman's fate is a loom,
a loom seen on old gravestones,
it is a winter night of untold stories.

I grew up an orphan, grew old a widow,
then grew to feel my shame.

A golden thread was falling from the sky,
Falling down, almost to earth.
Why does this gnaw at the heart?

From out of the ocean's depths
a wondrous fish swam forth,
it bore a ring of pearls
but could not swim to shore.
What storm howls in the breast?

Oh, to cry out—but no cries can come,
how pitiful, this beautiful earth!

4

If you are born on a doomed Monday,
don't even think of happiness:
you're lucky to escape at all
under your star of loss.

I was born on a doomed Monday
between Christmas and Epiphany,
when the old freezing cold bore down,
like a bear on linden stilts:
"Who's been cooking up my meat,
who's been winding my shaggy coat?"
The tiny stars were blinking,
unknown and unknowable all.

And I dreamed that I was loved,
that nothing was ever denied me,
that a golden comb smoothed my braids,
a silver sled bore me along,
and words from a secret book were read to me,
words that I soon forgot.

5

From the deepest well,
or the furthest star
my grandmother looks out from each thing:

Nothing, she says, nothing can we know.
We cannot say what we have seen.

We walk along, like two beggars.
Give us nothing, yet we are grateful.

Of the others, we know nothing.

6

If the world had master craftsmen,
they would build a chapel
over our miraculous well,
to replace what was once blown up . . .

If I had the slightest zeal,
I would sew you a cover of cloth,
showing Nicholas the Wonder Worker,
or anyone else you wanted . . .

If an angel would whisper in my ear
a word as beloved as evening stars,
held dear in the mind as it listens,
I would repeat it over and over
and know all that you seek—

Nothing is needed by the dead,
Not home, not clothing, not ears to listen.
They need nothing from us.
Nothing—except the wide, wide world.

7

All along the road, along the dusty road
I was walking and mourning, filled with grief—
you must know what it is to grieve. Do you?
When a stone shall swim as a fish,
then, I say, shall my soul
feel life and forgiveness.

The stone sails along like a boat,
blown by favorable winds,
righting its small gold sail,
its bright nettle-like wings,
its gold oars just barely glimpsed
in the distant, noisy sea.

And what was, will not be.
What will be is best of all.

8

Invisible flame, burn!
I need nothing else, only you.
All else will be taken from me.
If not taken, then I'll be asked to yield it.
If not asked, then I will cast it off,
out of boredom, and out of fear.

Like the star that gazes on the cradle,
or the watchhouse deep in the thicket,
swinging on the blackened chains,
burn, invisible flame, burn!

You are an icon lamp, oiled by tears,
by the doubt in a cruel heart,
by the smile of one who turns to leave.

So, burn, and pass along the news
to the Savior, to God in His Heavens,
that on earth He is remembered,
that He is still not forgotten.

9

(*A Prayer*)

Bring warmth, O Lord, to your Beloved flock—
the orphans, the infirm, the dispossessed.

For the one who can do nothing,
do all that he is bidden to do.

And for the dead, O Lord, the dead—
let their sins catch fire like straw,
let the sins burn and leave no trace
in the grave or the lofty heavens.

You are the Lord of all miracles and promises.
Let all that is not miracle burn away.

1982

POEMS ADDED TO "OLD SONGS"

DEDICATION

Remember, I say, remember,
remember, I say as I cry:
all will forsake, all will change,
and hope itself dies away.

The ocean does not fall into the river;
the river does not return to its source;
time has spared no one—

but I love you, I love you as if
all this were true, and yet may be.

Adam wept but was not forgiven.
And he was not allowed to return
to the only place where we are alive:

"If you want what is yours, you shall have it.
So what will you, you who are in that place
where the heart seeks as if God almighty:
where the heart is all radiance and offering."

The cold of the world—
someone will warm.

The deadened sun—
someone will raise.

These miracles—
someone will take by the hand,
like a naughty child, and say:

"Come, I will show you something
that you have never seen!"

1990-1992

TRISTAN AND ISOLDE

(Translated by Ksenia Golubovich & Caroline Clark)

FIRST INTRODUCTION

Pray listen, my good people,
to a story of love and death,
listen whoever wants to,
for it's within our every breath.
For the begging heart sends up such thanks
as if for its daily bread
when someone is lost,
when someone is dead,
or just as alone as we.

Let's sew a dress of darkness,
a monk's cloak of old,
let's ask for water from the well
and the northern winter's cold—
a winter lovely as topaz
though with a crack inside.
Like white topaz held to the eye,
when we lean to look outside
and into the streetlamp's light.

Fate alone is like fate
and unlike anything else:
not like the far distant sail,
not like a shield, a horn, or the Grail,
or whatever waits by the gate.
And those who know this are not sad
that light will go away like snow.

My soul, be whatever you want,
but be merciful too:
for here we come with life's knapsack,
lingering by the exit:
and I see that all fear the road.

Yet you will like them, those two,
who occupy my word.
We may have lived long ago, yet
like water hollowing the riverbed
when we speak it is always to say:
Pray listen to the living!

So when I start my speech, it seems
I am forever catching
at the passing hemline of a cloak,
and I seem to be always saying, "farewell,
you may not know me, but hear this:
like all the rest, I love."

And if all this is only death
and around me is only hell,
I'll still be kneeling before those knees,
still won't release my gaze.

And if I am to go on,
and close my eyes, forget my words,
unclench the hands of the mind,
that cloak will speak instead of me,
like my own blood inside.

And though I'll lie—don't interrupt:
for I know where I'm bound,
I know my hands are red with blood
and my heart lies underground.

But the light that was my very light,
and carried the third light high,
was the life of me, was the truth of me
and was more me than I.

SECOND INTRODUCTION

Where someone walks, someone looks
and thinks about him.
This look is open like a hollow
where a candle burns and waters flow
over a home that stands within.

Yet whoever decides that he's alone
in truth knows nothing at all,
he's not his own lord and master,
we'll speak of him no more.

But it is strange how a deed
sinks into the depths below
and there it lives like Lancelot
watching time pass overhead—
a wave rolling low.

I know not who has confused me,
or whose guilt I carry within,
but life is short, but life, my friend,
is a gift of glass that falls from the hand,
and death is long, like everything now,
and death is long, so long.

Ahead of it lies only water
and I am sorry a thousand times
that death must keep going on and on,
as though it weren't the horizon.

And joy comes up to its waist
and sorrow is ankle-high.

And when I fall asleep it is
my own voice that I hear:
"a single candle in your hand,
beloved, hold it near."

A single candle in her hand,
and downward it is turned,
as if both had raised their gaze
and passed without a word.

THIRD INTRODUCTION

A northern harp one last time
I shall take into my hands
and I'll kiss farewell, farewell
to that blind old music.
How I used to love that tune,
that light in love with the dark.

And nothing will end with itself,
as you once said to me—
not with evil, poison or slander,
or a wound of the heart's surrender,
not even death so young and tender
crossing above itself
two saplings in full bloom.

Dark is your storytelling,
yet it suddenly flares so bright
like a thousand colorful jewels
on a thousand slender hands,
and you see there's no one here:
and you see there is only light.

So let us ask that we may too
stay on here like light.
That we may build a house from tears
for everything we had to do
and remember day and night.

Go now, may the Lord be with you,
and eat your bread, your earthly path—
which leads I know not where, but away.
And night draws in behind you
a meadow colorful and heavy.

And if fate deals out to us
its most unlucky star,
the wind bloweth wherever it wills,
and we live wherever we are.

1. KNIGHTS RIDE TO THE TOURNAMENT

And so there can be times,
and such a time can be
when you sense the earth's heartbeat
and the smoke trailing thin—
the greenwood's earthy heartbeat
and glory's smoke so thin.
And the rest will hide away
behind a bush and a tree.

See the riders—how like the sun they are,
their horses made of the dark,
hoof and spear of a child's hurt,
and their shields of mystery.
They hurry to meet their Pentecost,
their holy day, their feast,
where death will fall like one young rose
upon an open breast.

Do you remember that same rose
looking in at us?
We try to hide our eyes away,
yet still it's looking in.

And the one who died young and loved,
and having loved himself,
walked and all that was ahead of him,
he touched and turned to living gold—
like Midas, only happier.

And now he is everywhere
and he is that very dream
that the hillside sees and horizon sees,
all those skies that are bright like him
and glorified like him.

Now life is overgrown,
the forests are too dense,
and speech is hard and it's hard for me
to draw the veil of spirits and shades
away with my own hand.

Some wear black, some lilac,
some scarlet or heavenly blue,
but they ride and ride
and are looking
to where the rose is splashing awash
in the narrow ladle of legends.

2. BEGGARS WALK THE ROAD

O, how I want to love the Lord,
just as His paupers do.
I want to walk the towns
and plead in His name true,
to learn it all and then forget,
to start to talk like the dumb or dead
of His sweet beauty too.

You think a candle stands here,
and that Lent is a quiet garden?
But if it is a garden, they will enter
and perhaps won't find any faith within,
and candles spin no happiness here
but ruefully hang down.

And therefore you must close your door
and bury your clear mind:
it will spring up if alive,
whilst you must lie and wait behind.
And follow or bring inside
whoever wants to enter.
Don't pick or choose between them:
a horrible sight they all are,
like worms on a wheel they all are.

And what if they kill me?
Then let that be too:

you'll be given your medicine—
a few drops of blue.
And if my home is burned?
          —So let it fall
for it isn't your home at all.

3. A SHEPHERD PLAYS

In a heraldic garden small
vines begin to bloom.
"Here we come!"
from a window they call,
and fourteen merry goat kids
leap over a flute.

Yes, they leap over a flute,
or they bound over a pipe,
no animals more charming
has anyone ever seen.
The Lord stinted the rest.
Their fur is the best,
as bold as a youthful abyss—
looking, breathing and stirring,
filling the heart with bliss.

Yet in every living man
the heart is dark and poor,
he is a cripple all inside:
come what may—who cares,
he will not sit down with us
dressed in proper clothes
to serve the blooming vines
to his merry goat kids.

Just as the Lord bids.

4. SON OF THE MUSES

Strange images and pictures
will enter through closed doors,
will find their own names
and something for me to do.
They'll pour my simple reason
just like sand onto the shore,
rock it like a cradle,
or weave it into a basket.
And they will ask:
what do you see?
And I shall say:
all I can see
are waves beating the shore.

Waves beating without end,
for a lofty wave is a chest
for the best and most beautiful ring
and a cellar for wine, the best.
Let the deep swallow its visions
or let it rumble like a furnace,
it will carry us out—

But where?
Wherever we happen to go,
wherever we are told.
But where, my spirit, but where?
O, how should I know?

The abyss is better than a shepherd
at tending its own flocks:
visible to no one
they climb all over the hills
and play there like the stars.
Their constant ringing,
their milky way,
scatters like mercury far away
and then comes back to us:

For poor are folk, and scant is our tale,
for all end here, and the world has long forgotten us.

As Policrates threw his ring
to whatever was meant to be—
whoever was poor,
whoever was rich,
whoever waged wars,
or tended calves—
the most precious
of all these things
is the one smallest grain flying *back*.

So take your ring, Policrates,
you have lived your life in vain.
Whoever throws out the most
will be loved by people the most.
In blackened sores and in his sins
he is like those smoky hearths
with the same old fire, the same old glint
of the heavens' merry crackle.

And the waves beat, they know no end,
for a lofty wave is a chest
for the best and most beautiful ring
and a cellar for wine, the best.
When the deep swallows its visions,
we will say:
there's nothing to lose!
And the deep will say that's so.

And the dead are not embarrassed
by a strange and meager zeal—
they whisper in his ear
all that he forgot.
Having said goodbye to torment,
they crowd around the doors

with stories like those
they tell on Christmas Eve—
of gold and pearls and of the light
that comes out of nothing.

5. A BRAVE FISHERMAN
A peasant song

Can you hear, mama, a bird that is singing?
Wings beating in a cage, it doesn't drink or feed.

A fisherman once said to me
when I was going home:
take a double chain with you
and take my golden ring,
for the night is short
and spring is short
and the river takes the boats.

I bowed to him low
and then I said to him:
the double chain I'll take, my lord,
I will not take the ring,
for the night is short
and spring is short
and the river takes the boats.

Ah, mama, I keep dreaming:
some snow and smoke I see,
and a sinful soul is crying
before a blessed angel,
for the night is short
and spring is short
and the river takes the boats.

6. A WOUNDED TRISTAN DRIFTS IN A BOAT

Magnificence burns bright,
like a pearl dissolved
in a pitched and darkened bottle.
Yet in the depths of earthly hurts,
it starts to speak like a mighty wave,
like ancient Pontus unsurpassed.

O, my deathly longing, you want
to rise like a seawall from the fog,
to embrace yourself from far away
with the hands of the ocean.
Now with Bran's silver wand
and the prophetic cry of the reed
confusing what we hear,
for ages you have been learning,
that like a sweetly aching wound,
life is vast at parting.

I like Tristan when from the tower
he jumps into the sea:
his deed is really like a star.
How else can we run from grief
but with courage purer then water?
I like the blood from a deep wound,
how it adorns every caress.
Que faire? I like an epilogue

where the ocean can be heard,
I love its every mask.

O, drift like wounded Tristan,
plucking at restless strings,
playing the music of free suffering
up to the heavens where a hurricane roams.

And within the vast ocean's longing
the hero's hushed yearning
is like a hamlet beneath a mountain,
like a household that's early to bed,
outside a blizzard blowing.

And the blizzard gazes like a pale beast
through a thousand eyes of lashes
watching people sleep, while craftswomen
spin the common flax,

and of the ancient Fleece of Colchis
fate's spindle whirs its tale.

"We shall not find it."
"It matters not."

7. A CONSOLATION DOG

Accept, my friend, a consolation dog,
a lovely dog, a thing of beauty.
It's made of nothing and all its traits
are rainbows: unfailing bridges
over a rivulet of simple music—
you'll soon know it by heart.
There floating by is your new, eternal wreath:
buds of candles, flowers of torches.

How this reminds me of fortune-telling,
when they knock at the embers:
sparks fly out
and are counted,
but as in a dream,
when
they
freely spread out
their painted sails.
Yet it's not the winds that drive them,
but unknown voices.

These ships are ancient, rowing ships.
Their wine-gold oceans
carry us to consolation,
along the merry, lofty isles
stored up for a happier life,
on tender, cutting waves.

What is the roar of waves telling us?
And what is the Nereid saying?
It's as if someone is thanking us,
keeping a hold of our hand:
"Onward, my poor wanderers!
The bottom of life is simple:
a clean cloth pulled tight
across an embroidery frame."

It's not in vain that we walk the hungry deep
as though around the house.
Here reverie embroiders in gold,
and the unforgettable paints
its pictures and names onto a wave:

here is the ball of childhood,
here the lovers' tryst,
and this is simply a winter's day.
Here is music framed by a filigree
of nighttime bushes and villages.
Such precious work. Forget it.
And further on: a lime tree.
The lime tree by the city gates.
And Christmas.

And now—there's nothing to see.
Yet this is the best thing to see.

And when, however much a shame,
we too will be no more,

we shall surely find ourselves
somewhere quite close to this . . .

Accept, my friend, a gift of my deep sorrow.
For beauty is much stronger than our hearts.
It is a fortune-teller's cup—
the most translucent vessel for the incredible.

8. THE KING AT THE HUNT

My horse where art thou taking me?
Take me wherever thou will.
My soul is armored safe,
and life is ever free

to rule over itself
and hunt with fierce dogs,

to make cures with eastern potions,
or deal out maladies,

to feed itself in secret
on bears' and foxes' milk,

or lie between two lovers
like an old, unblemished sword.

And if—most strange and distant dream—
she stands before me pure?
Not that she is faithful, but because
you can't exhaust
the depths,
can't comprehend
the heights;
whoever's gone beyond Hades's gates
will never come back, at least
that's what they say.

O, woman's will is rude and coarse,
she has no fear, she is
an unrelenting slave . . .
Deer,
my friend,
run on, if it be fate
for you to escape . . .
Yes, rude and coarse and knows
everything once and for all.

Weakening, meanwhile—
that is *our* handiwork.

9. A DWARF TELLS FORTUNES BY THE STARS
(and also about leprosy)

O leprosy, all ancient horror
can fit into this one thing alone.
Immortality itself seems to sink
like a stone at the very sight of it:
can the heavens cause such offense
that a man will hate another man
as he does his own death?

Yet evil which no eye can see
is more abysmal than leprosy.

The worthiest man visits lepers
and cleans their wounds with tender hands
and serves them as a miser does his gold:
they're bounty for such holy hearts.
And he carries their shame with him,
as the ocean carries a hollow canoe,
and rocks,
and shifts, and moves around,
and does as God has bid . . .

But who will help one who is wicked,
when he gnaws at another's life
like a dog with a stolen bone?
Why does he understand the stars?
They fall to pieces, part, divide.
All love this clustering—but not him.

He is like a nail driven into himself.
Who digs such nails out?

Who'll bring him medicine and sit
at his bedside? Who is
the doctor that will, without revulsion,
treat his guile and envy?
Maybe shame alone—
and the dwarf too knows this.

He pushes away each constellation
and asks for retaliation.

(The evil once done by us,
now, with the same secret lust
it always grew on, feeds
on self-immolation):

"I am, but may I be made
like something not yet made,
and you will read the pure light of suffering
in me, just as I read the stars!"

And he broke free from the deepest dark
to a new and different sky,
from the gloom that would but growl and bark,
being what it was: himself, his I.

10. NIGHT
Tristan and Isolde meet a hermit in the woods

> *Love, hunter of hearts,*
> *is tightening its bow,*
> *how oft it seemed to me*
> *that life's but a short sound:*
> *it is like a worn sack*
> *stuffed with fiery groats,*
> *and a narrowing aim.*

Through a hedge of roses reaching its hands again,
a story most beautiful nurtures such pain

whose sweetness is unrivaled: a weighty almandine
is rolling through the leaves, alone and not alone.

What excites our mind beyond its very limits?
That which promises the thing our mind prohibits:

the soul runs from itself and sees an example in you—
o never-resting Ahasver, the ever-wandering Jew.

Hiding from my one and only solace,
from the blood on the thorns of a mysterious fence:

it's not pleasure I want: such things my mind ignores,
like that Eternal Jew, demanding something more . . .

But here we have a story where for all time
fateful pain is rustling, like an ancient lime.

With Mistress Death hidden under leaf
their vast night grows from day's wreath,

it grows and says that life is not enough—
life longs for more and grips itself above

the abyss. And now broken into pieces,
it will grow back together as the longing increases.

So in the woods they still embrace each other,
the dog keeps guard, while hunger pushes them further

to the end. And in that wood where their fear reeled
lived a hermit, like a lark above a field.

He gave them honey and roots for food
and with these alms let them go for good—

like two who'd lost their house to fire, found adrift
and then left alone. He had the strangest gift:

to see in the heart's heights all triumph over loss,
Our Lord of Joy who hangs upon the cross.

11. A MILL WHIRS

O, happiness, you are simple,
you are a simple cradle,
a basket woven from willow,
a fir tree in the wind.
And if we are to perish,
you'll be our only end.
Like all others in the world,
I can see as before
a crack full of light
from under a closed door.

O, life has no meaning.
O, the mind, like the heart, it aches.
Far away a child is crying,
and a mill whirs and scrapes.
That's the haircloth of hearing,
the thin dust of bread.
And the corn screams like a bird
inside the heavy millstones.
And a voice that is solitary, simple and far
is talking to Vesper, the first star.

O Lord, my dear Master,
forgive me if you can.
And if you can, then let my heart
go free, be at liberty:
forgotten and unneeded,
no use to anyone,

to descend a huge staircase
into the dark so vast,
and toss life like a golden ball,
invisible to the mind.

Where we can vanish and see as before
a crack of light from under a closed door.

O, tell me, my sweet darling,
what do we live for in this world?
To hear a child's crying
and to serve the stars.
And the stars are looking down
from their caves or deep abyss:
that must be him, son of the tsar,
he, too, is waiting and alone,
he, like them, is alone.

And some strange force, like water,
that plashes beneath the ice
looked through the stars
that look down here
from their highest heights.

And its likeness—empty, solitary and far—
will turn out to be the first and brightest star.

12. THE HERMIT SPEAKS

May the Lord protect you,
as he protects us all.
Inside this rough and empty life
lies a treasure as if buried in a field.
And above it a tree speaks
such words of happiness.

And the sky takes a deep bow
in the shape of flying birds:
they can fill the eye-sockets
with miraculous milk.
O, it's possible to think of no one,
and no one to forget.

I now choose an image
that resembles me:
the creak of a forest at night,
the noise of a rainy day,
a path where someone walks
and sees there drifting before him
an unexpected and shaky raft
of the last flames.

May the Lord protect you,
the Lord who reads our hearts
in melancholy, disgrace,
and the abyss of the end and fall—

inside the closed casket's glass,
ever out of reach:

where the simple will to be
is crying like a child,
may the Lord protect you,
like the purest gold,
His own.

1978-1982

IN PRAISE OF POETRY

(Translated by Caroline Clark)

Dear Vladimir Arkadievich,

Your suggestion that I write about the circumstances surrounding my earliest poems initially dismayed me:

first, it is not done to talk of such private matters;

second, only historical things have a prehistory—and perhaps only Goethe in his old age or the author of Doctor Faustus *could properly write* Poetry and Truth *or* The Story of a Novel;

third, this is no foolproof matter: one risks dismantling a music box that may yet have something more to play,

last, one must be at least a little self-satisfied in order to recall anything at all: the past fades away when faced with the chastising present. And it is in that same present that I happen to be.

Nevertheless I have written these notes, without plan or agenda, confusing happenings with imaginings, omitting a great deal, and intertwining much that is superfluous.[6]

It is with gratitude that I dedicate them to you—"a friend in the generation" of many living poets, that "reader in posterity"[7] for which every poet hopes, and an expert on our First Poet.[8]

IN PRAISE OF POETRY

I have been making up poems since before I can remember. My mother wrote to my father—in China, I believe—telling him how I was learning to speak in rhyme, and she added: "Maybe she'll be a poet."[9] When secretly reading other people's letters (something I swear I have not done for a long time), I was never able to make them out in full, through to the end. Something like a surge of conscience would tug them away from my eyes like a third hand, and a kind of fear would rearrange the letters. And so I could read only the rhyme: "Nina—seen her."

Unlike my young mother, I know that children often learn words through rhyme and that this has nothing to do with poetry. I find the idea of poets having a predominantly aural awareness to be exaggerated ("For the poet only sound is important," as is often quoted from Trediakovsky).[10] And I consider the call to

> Evoke as sound in my heart
> What you cannot express in words

to be a most cunning means of retreat. But I will tell you later on, when the time comes, what I think about poetry.

My sister Irina had either not yet been born or had only just been born. In one of the first poems that I remember, it was the discrepancy between reality and the way I represented it that assured the poem's success among adults:

> Spring has come
> To us in the yard.
> My sister has climbed
> Up onto the fence.

(Then I used my hands and feet, rather than words, to show how she "fell off the fence and ended up in a hole.")

> Oh where am I?
> And where's my yard?
> And where's my spring?
> And where's my fence?

Here is another poem from my preschool years:

> Not being a person
> I then thinked:
> What do we need these rivers for
> And why is there water in them?
> But being a person,
> I now think:
> We do need these rivers
> And the water in them too.

I don't know what I meant by "Not being a person." Being *who* exactly? But I could see those rivers, regardless of the water, as clearly then as I do now. I understood that the repetition must be total, or rather: any one thing that happens must be sure to involve everything else mentioned. And so, with the fence lost and gone, spring would just have to disappear too. The world is nowhere as whole as in stanzaic form. Elena Shvarts also writes about this:

> Bind now this whole world
> with a chain of similes,
> otherwise it will melt
> and fade into the soundless ether.[11]

It never seemed to me that anything depended on similes alone or on poetry in general. On the contrary, I saw poetry as an infinitely dependent thing, almost completely expended by its dependency— but on what? On the disposition of the stars, the condition of one's liver, a rumbling underground? I cannot say. I love the fateful in poetry, although you may be surprised to hear which lines I find particularly fateful. For example:

> Midst golden fields and greenest pastures
> The lake spreads blue and broad;
> Across its unknown waters
> A fisherman drifts . . .[12]

Perhaps because this is no longer a lake but the sky, or because there is nothing like this on earth, nor could there ever be—and yet this is all there is. In short, I cannot say why these lines used to make me hysterical. I would have the urge to break something, if only a dish. I could see the fate "of Sophocles, not of Shakespeare" (as Akhmatova said on quite a different occasion)[13] descending upon us like a bird of prey, perhaps like the eagle to Ganymede, with this blue, green and gold landscape of the Unknown. To me, fully incarnate poems are fateful.

But despite making up rhymes all through my school years, the strange thing is that I had no idea about the inexpressible content that compels one to be a poet. It was pure poetastery, graphomania without the slightest inspiration, without a hint of simple sincerity. I never wrote about what excited me: I did not think this was *allowed*. For me the words "allowed" and "not allowed" decided everything. Anything that was not allowed was hateful and not to be desired. While doing my schoolwork I would place a portrait of Lenin in front of me. I needed a supervisor, better still—the *author* of those orders I was performing, for only the author could appraise my performance and reward me with his approval. Without any real or imagined praise (in the way, for example, this gilded portrait changed his expression) I would not do anything. In addition to having these traits of a fawner and prig, so unnatural for a poet, there was one more. I was inarticulate and unable to construct grammatically coherent sentences. Many people lack this ability, but not to such an extent. Alarmed by my severe inability to "express thoughts," my parents would make me paraphrase books. This did not help: I simply learned whole paragraphs and sections by heart and repeated them. In the meantime a grammatical idiocy flourished. I found constructing my own normal sentences somewhat crude and dishonest, as if by articulating the theme and rheme and connecting everything by case and number, I was slipping into someone else's dress—and an ugly one at that.[14] Many people feel ill at ease when hearing inflated or stilted language, but for me all connected speech was inflated in this way.

And so, sincerity and plausibility in poems were not to be "allowed." Anyone who understands the full force of this word will know that asking *why* can have no bearing here. I do not wish to justify my graphomania, but at the heart of this delusion lies good sense. There is, I feel, a type of sincerity or truth about oneself that when professed becomes a slander against the whole world. The spoken and heard word does not exist in order to articulate, repeat or, still less, reveal anything—and this includes the one speaking it. This word—by virtue of its own sound and its unpredictable ability to mean something else, something more than that with which it is to be entrusted—strives to *enrobe*. I need not, of course, explain to you that to enrobe is not to mask or refresh the paint on the whited sepulchers;[15] it is not to conceal something truly bad under an unreal or pseudo-real goodness. Let us agree that we know what it is to enrobe. Otherwise I fear I shall become another author of *Selected Passages* failing, at that, to write my "Government Inspector."[16]

True, there was one exception to this exemplary insincerity: before going to sleep I would make up poems about death, but I never wrote them down or considered them to be poems. The idea of death first entered my head when I was about seven, in the first grade. It was not a thought, but a hole, not in my head or in my chest, but somewhere in my stomach. Once there, this hole settled inside my consciousness and from time to time everything would be drawn into it with a whistling sound, and there would be nothing left behind. I do not know where it came from—maybe general talk about a nuclear war. I understood that this thought was somehow unseemly and did not speak of it. Immortality, something I had heard about in passing, did not blot out this thought and did not command that same force of tangible presence as "death," "never," and particularly "never again." I had also heard of paradise, which to me was like a cherry tree that, like those rivers without water, was made up only of the marks and features of a cherry tree. And paradise related to everything that was *other than* death—a thing that, even in all its entirety, paradise could not outweigh. This Arzamas terror[17] persisted for months and eventually ended of its own accord. Having observed my dreadful unprovoked fits of crying a hundred times a day, my grandmother asked an old woman from the church to come, and together they said some prayers and sprinkled holy water over me. They were probably exorcising demons—the midnight and midday demons of mortal despair. Maybe it ended because the holidays were over and there was no time for that sort of thing at school. But when the fear did come over me, I would hush it and, before going to sleep, make up lines that I did not think of as poetry and that, for some reason, calmed me:

> In this cold country
> It will be cold.
> Then everyone will forget about me
> And I will forget where the people are.

They calmed me in that they proved to be at least somehow effable. I learned only many years later that before writing a poem (whatever the subject and however sunny the words and resonance of the words may be) one must have the same sense of fear as when faced with this chilling lullaby. The same, and yet, not exactly the same, of course . . .

As for an early experience of *others'* mortality, I am indebted to a children's story, one that gave rise to a sudden sense of vitality that came slanting toward me in a strange light. It is not for me to say here whether it was a good story. It was about a boy's grandmother who died. He would always answer back and sulk with her when she was alive, but he suddenly realizes just *what it is* that he has lost. Though that's not the point. The point is that he finds a list she wrote—she never did learn to put the right number of strokes in the letter *u*—and this sets him off crying. With words I use today, I can now more or less explain what his crying was about: there is a certain point after which everything is good, not just good, but it delights you—why? Because it goes on existing even when faced with the horror of its inevitable absence. The force of this point knocked me out. It was like a spear striking a center that apparently determined whether we can live "like other people" or not: that is, do your lessons, answer the question put to you, sip your tea. This point performed its task unerringly no matter when it came to mind, never weakening from repetition. But the problem was not only this incapacitating point, so unexpectedly discovered. It was also that the *living thing* and the *imperfect thing* came to be bound up for me in an irresolvable oneness. To die meant to never be alive again and to never be imperfect at, say, writing the letter *u*. And as for perfection itself becoming impossible—that was the least of my worries. But above all: it is precisely imperfection that needs burning love—not an indulgent love, but one that makes you ashamed, if only for you to be aware of this imperfection. As such, there is no place for any other attitude because, as we know, there are no perfect things on earth. There are things that excel themselves, but none that are perfect. So that's that. This is one reason why I love literature. One moment we might not notice anything at all but, having read the right story, we will for ever after be aware of what the author saw—and even more if we try.

And so I would make up stock verses and show them right away. It was important that the ending of the poem met with approval; even today I do not think this is a bad thing. Chesterton has a charming idea about how vanity is closer to humility than to shrewd modesty. This is surely true: vanity is more defenseless. For me the most important characteristic of a poem was that it be written in another language. Sometimes I wrote using the Latin alphabet, seeing as this was the only foreign thing I knew, for example:

RUSALKI
Svetit luna
Noчka temna
Bliki vody na reke
Tuчki plyvut
Zvëzdy pojut
Roща stoit vdaleke.[18]

(MERMAIDS
Shine moon
Dark night
Sparkly river
Clouds float by
Stars sing
Faraway in the wood.)

The more incomprehensible, the more I liked it. For example:

Apollo triumphant on Olympus
Will raise up an immortal from the mortals.[19]

I could not understand a single word of this and so memorized it with special determination. Apart from this poem by Delvig, before starting school other poems I memorized and recited to guests were: "My mother sang to me," "Wise Prince Oleg roused to arms," the lyrics of "Over the valleys and hilltops"[20] that I had learned with my grandmother from the almanac (a tear-off calendar), and one poem from which I now remember only a single verse:

Lord have mercy
On the wretched orphan
Give him joy and strength
Be a tower of strength for him!

And many others like it from the parish school syllabus that my grandmother would recite to me:

Proud thy nape did'st not bend
In thy fateful destiny.
And shall the stepchildren of Russia
Not bow to thee?[21]

Old Slavonic words particularly thrilled me. It was precisely their quasi-intelligibility that I felt distinguished the language of poetry. This meant, in the first place, that I should use words that are never used in real life. In the second: I should write poems similar to those already written, because these alone were poems. The closer I got, the prouder I was. For example, like Zhukovsky:

The plain is beautiful, full of flowers,
It lives, breathes, and trembles.

(I was particularly proud of my use of "breathes" here).[22] Third: I should observe rhyme and meter. This then was the sum of my creative tasks between the ages of seven and fourteen. And of course poems were also supposed to be about something clever.

Keeping to a regular meter was not difficult. Iambic lines of varying length were, I believed, a result of Krylov's tin ear.[23] To my mind, any original turn came from the author's ineptitude. Which is, in part, fair. I still believe that if Nekrasov had had a talent for refined verse like that of Pushkin, as Lermontov had (and we know from his debut how things stood),[24] he would not have found his own unusual lyric form. The Formalists' "struggle against the automatization of the device"[25] often means nothing more than: "necessity is the mother of invention." The idea that something can be "automatized," "banal," and "obsolete" arises only when looking at literature from the outside, which excludes not only judgment and opinion but any value, too. To do this (to speak of the obsolete) one must set the first (value-based) use on par with the second, and even the tenth appearance of the device. In its first and real appearance, it is not a device at all and thus cannot be automatized no matter how its empty likeness is exploited by contemporaries, later writers, or the author himself. Nevertheless, the conscientious epigone is always faced with the first thrilling appearance of that resplendent weapon—one which is only capable of yielding a single victory, but which he wants to use again, hoping that it will prove to be "immortal" or non-automatizable.

Meanwhile however, childhood, having disappeared without a trace amid this painstaking epigonic gibberish, consisted entirely of a profound and mysterious poetry. For some time now the poetic viewpoint has been associated with that of the child: Rilke, Khlebnikov and Pasternak, among others, were influential in establishing this. The poetic nature of Pushkin, by comparison, has nothing in common with a child's point of view. Many great lyric poets write from the point of view of youth. These "childlike" poets usually present more difficulty for the reader precisely because they are simpler: they choose the shortest path of expression for certain things, the most direct way, not yet drawn out by later circumstances. It works like this: you can only get from point A to point B via C, which is off to one side. Why? Because the bus won't go any other way. You can only get from object to object (metaphor) via this route—the one that our mind is used to taking. And in the same way—from assumption to deduction, etc.

It is true, though, that the things spoken about so directly by these "child's view" poets inevitably concern that which either has been forgotten, or was never understood, or is impossible to reach by any sort of bus. For the A and B of art are located, after all, in the air and are accessible only by aerial ways: it's best to get there by flying. The same poets are usually also metaphysical; or rather they are mostly interested in the "nature of things" (love poetry or the hero with his tale are not for them). Childhood is occupied with the "nature of things," trying to match names to things. And it must somehow cope with the enormous variety of unique things and the pull of even the smallest of them to become unique. And when a phenomenon—floating and immeasurable, delicate and immense, like a cloud of pollen—suddenly folds its wings like a butterfly and settles, becoming a "wooden trunk" or "winter" for example—and leaves in its wake the possibility for new and completely different wings to open, to fly away and be given a new name or no name at all—this moment inspires a sense of elation such that the triumph of good over evil, let's say, could never bring. This is an exclusively cognitive ethics, provided that what we call "cognition" means initiation in unique, life-giving, miraculous meaning; and on the condition that this initiation comes from above and is not gained by force. It may be that from these years onward the amount of the past only grows less: back when we are small it is clear that *everything* has already happened to us (if only because even the tiniest thing is undeniably a part of *everything*), and this "has already" in no way differs from "will be"—just as it should be with the real past. This is all between the ages of three and four.

Let these stories not perpetuate the sentimental cult of child-hood, which is so tiresome and springs entirely from the boredom of adults. Being an adult is more interesting still, for transformed nature is more precious and rewarding than that with which we are born. Saint Augustine was no child, and no child wrote Beethoven's sonatas! Be it deed or creation, it is all the same: *Der Weg von der Innigkeit zur Größe geht durch das Opfer.*[26] But a child has nothing to offer up as a sacrifice, for everything it has is blissfully another's. And later on, what is it that we can have as our "own"? Ah, nothing of any good. Only the futile possibility to reject this thing that is our own (which we cannot do when left to ourselves). For holding onto our "own" is more fearsome than the act of rejecting it. Victor Aksyuchits writes something similar in his explanation of the fall of man, but with more optimism than I can muster.[27]

But let's return to where I started, with this thing that is blissfully another's, this gift to which we still cling. That same quasi-butterfly will reappear: here it is in a phrase read to you for the first time (but what seems to be the second), and it turns into a bed covered with a red blanket in the depths of a room; a wooden trunk reveals the wings of an encounter, and hanging above it in the dark corridor is a fur coat smelling of mothballs and snow; a cherry tree takes shape outside the dacha window in the form of a musical phrase. These old and unnamed acquaintances do not emerge fully formed at the tug of a single characteristic, as in Proust (and they were not fully them-selves even then). They were choked-back tears, heavy like a blanket, or like a gleaming pillar of dust in the chest, or "the whistling of yearning which did not start with me," as Pasternak said.[28] They were not here, before my eyes, but rather, there behind my back—or, better yet: in place of me.

So as not to indulge in the illusion of the angelic or Adamic nature of the child's soul, we should ask: was there room in it for another person? This was not a peopleless world; rather, people were something different from what they later came to be. It was as though they were the direct speech of everything else, everything non-human. When a room, having gathered all its strength, addressed me in such a way that I could not fail to understand—it was my grandmother. The river and trees spoke with the voice of my mother. Everything far beyond the window was my father, roughly speaking. But the presence and absence of these "words" was not so clear-cut: like, for instance, when it is not possible to fully separate direct speech from a message communicated to us by an interlocutor. There are the unchanging features of his face and his changing expression, his height, etc. Because the main message communicated is his very self (or herself). And this "himself-itself-herself" of infancy could either speak to us or be silently present; but to distance itself or leave us—this it could not do.

Yuri Tynianov says that Pasternak (an exemplary "child's view" poet) provides us with a connection to things that did not previously exist. It did exist, I assure you. There were as many connections as you could wish for; back then nothing had properly come undone yet. The "it itself"—something whole—clearly reigns over all separate things, each of which is only a momentary contraction of this whole: something omnipresent that is concentrating and compressing itself into the burning bush of a thing's image. This miracle would not amaze a child. No kind of shape shifting can amaze a child, not even the shifting from "everything" to "one of." And vice versa. There are not just the two obvious components in similes and metaphors: more important is a third and more general element in which their affinity lies, the milieu of their contact, the grand total of their sameness. I speak of that very *whole* whose reality becomes apparent in the most miraculous of metamorphoses. Any simile essentially speaks of this whole:

> The call and response of the steamboat
> With another far-off steamboat.[29]

—and not of the qualification of one unknown by another that is no better known.

And since this one common thing (this he-she-it) was glad to receive us and existed especially for us, it tried to be beautiful for the time of our arrival: all its movements and words were beautiful and differed little one from another, for they came together in beauty.

Apart from familiar words—of relatives and my nanny—there were also mysterious people: children. They were entirely other to me. In very early childhood they all seemed to be more important, interesting, and beautiful than I was, because they could disappear: they had a secret. Their homes, food, and clothes were a part of this secret. I did not have a secret like this, and I was always entirely at my own disposal. Neither my nanny nor grandmother would call me in from the window and lead me away from myself. In the "other," there was a different and better world, as any other world was. It did not occur to me to try to possess this secret, for I loved it devotedly as a secret. Each stranger had the ability to turn into a "charming demon,"[30] into a treasure—"and the key was entrusted only to me."[31] And here is one, maybe the first, such delightful demon: a girl called Oksana in a meadow at Valentinovka. We were two years old, still unable to speak very well, and so we communicated by other means. She had chestnut locks (her beauty enhanced by the fact that my head was shaved clean) and the blackest eyes. The absence of any non-black color in those eyes can only be likened to a panther—I remind you of the third component in similes. And this absolute blackness shone. This is how I imagine the eyes of the biblical Rachel. We probably met throughout the summer on the meadow, but I remember it as one encounter, brief and cut short by those who led her away. She was not, of course, distressed by our separation: for her, blessed with such perfection, what was a separation from me? I howled like a wounded animal and was left forever with the memory of this beauty having already turned away, leaving me—like the famous figure (was it Spring?) in Pompeii frescoes. She has no choice but to leave and not be doomed to remain here where nothing will tolerate her boldness. She must leave, like the utterly incarnate, the eternal leaving the ephemeral, and she inspires sorrow about the eternal and the ephemeral and about everything of this world. But there is nothing sweeter than this sorrow; it is like a "yes" spoken with a gesture of negation. Today the same boldness of beauty possessed by that unknown Oksana seems to me to be cast forth by the shadow of another boldness I have encountered—the poetic boldness of Elena Shvarts.

Now, imagining myself back then, I understood even then that the state of being in love dreams of insurmountable obstacles; it nurtures within itself all external impossibilities: all nannies coming to lead you away, all the indifference of the beloved, the faithful husband and the evil dwarf (as the story of Tristan and Isolde shows). This movement that is so precisely trained on its target does not, after all, want a target. It is not much easier for me to explain now than it was then. If I can rephrase a simile from a poem by Leonid Aronzon, it is a butterfly bearing its own candle.[32] Some things tell us that nothing is completely "from here"; the state of being in love tells us that indeed nothing is completely here and that everything is heading toward the "not-here."

Oksana has somehow managed to take up too much room here, and no less would be needed for various other bits and pieces: the sandpit, lanterns, floorboards, and especially the sledge. I remember how I would be taken home from the tram, all wrapped up and strapped in, and anyone with a harsh voice would leave behind a big track. The snow fills the air, the darkness creaks, everything is now a dream, now laughter . . . It might seem that childhood, like dreams (and like visions used to be), is an important subject no matter how it is told. But this is simply a mistake. There are no subjects of this kind at all. And if it seems to you that everyone should share your excitement at the mere mention of all these things—be assured: they pine and yearn because they feel they ought to share your intimate excitement, yet are incapable of doing so. And so I have left out various things and happenings—the mere list of them is like a profound and intricate poem to me—off-stage: may they live there, become friends, shimmer and not resent me. God willing we will meet again some day, perhaps when I come up with a way to talk about them.

Besides the poetry of things and people that snows down generously over our childhoods (and which many of us later remember as being like an endearing mistake, or the delightfully faltering speech of a baby's first babble, or the fog that charmingly distorts the present, unpoetic state of things), I had the rare luck to hear the poetry of language. It was my grandmother who spoke this poetic Russian language. The prosaic kind was completely foreign to her. There were wake-up songs, lullabies, nursery rhymes, and folk sayings for every unforeseeable event in life. She said them in a low voice, full of wonder and with no trace of tiredness ("my strong old voice is doing well," she would say):

"Do you know what the cat's purring?"

> Pawing and purring
> It's time for raking
> Haystack shaking
> No time for breaking
> When your back's aching
> Pawing and purring.

But the point is not these ready-made singsong rhymes. I do not doubt that she came up with them on the spot and nothing she ever said sounded any worse than sayings worn smooth by centuries' use. This was not what distinguished her speech or any speech that I love from a dead "literary" language (these quotation marks are to keep real literary language beyond reproach: it can be more alive than any vernacular or dialect; the quotation marks are for that approximate literary language that exists in the minds of editors). What is the good of any "tarns" and "denes" if together they lack that astute tension or insight that we find in the eloquent speech of common people and great poets? Behind "literary" language, which resembles the rules of a game without an object, lies a disregard of reality. One of the main rules of this language is that there is nothing worth staying silent about, and there are no things for which some word or other cannot be used. Behind my grandmother's speech was a sense she was always keeping an eye on things and an ear to things. There was her way of thinking and working things out whatever the occasion—and her way of keeping silent when there was nothing to say (while "literary" language always thrives in these places). These were not words but names: unique and, like names (in the so-called mythological mentality), they were difficult to get out of things. But once out, they took a firm hold—if only so as to play with them and wash them clean like the dishes at the end of "Fedora's Grief."[33]

There was Grandmother sorting grain on the table in the garden and threatening the wind, which kept blowing everything away from her:
  "Hey, armless!"
  "Why armless?"
  "Because he's flying head first without looking."

She would speak as though not conscious of her words—and the result was an unconscious originality. Not the type that is built up like a second floor over the conscious and immediately concealed banality of the first words to enter the mind, but an originality of *direct* speech: the originality of the pre-verbal world itself, in which it would be laughable to suspect anything banal.

◆

I remembered once more about what poetry was at the end of my school years. Someone read me a poem written by a ninth-grade fellow schoolgirl:

> I will come to your wedding in black,
> The devil will be your bridegroom.
> . . . .
> . . . . (*I don't remember*)
> I'll break a bottle on the table:
> Sweet to see how it flows.
> That same force might crack
> My skull tomorrow.

I fear that everything turned out just as imagined here for this girl whose name I no longer remember. For some things are never said in vain. And what I remembered once more about poetry is this: poetry deals with the other, something I do not deny, but this other (unlike the other of the epigone with which I was then familiar) had that same passion for reality as so-called life. More even, in fact:

stark ist dein Leben, doch dein Lied ist stärker.[34]

It is easy to forget all this if one only thinks of poetry as nineteenth-century verse, which concealed its beguiling sense, the sense of the powerful deed, behind what was already a poorly understood form. Or as verse from 1960s periodicals that never had any such sense. That line, "Sweet to see how it flows," stunned me more than any declaration made by a poet I knew (true, there were not many of them). Everything this line spoke of was still to come; it would happen to me or in my presence. While the answer to the challenge set by Pushkin or Baratynsky was already in the past.

Why necessarily a challenge? Why not a "soothing balm"?[35] Because, as I hope to relate later, the "soothing balm" of poetry, the evensong within its reach, the grateful consent or blessing, are but aspects of the general sense of this challenge. In the first place, people have arranged their social lives so that nothing poetic would arise in them: such are rules of community life, of upbringing, etc. But this is not the main thing. There is reason enough for the lyric poet to be surrounded by a halo of tragedy or suffering; there is reason enough that the thought of a poet should bring to mind an early or fatal demise. Every preconception has its grounds, particularly one that is generally accepted. Who else wears such a halo? "The noble man," the hero. Lyric poetry—as I hope to set forth later in more detail, if

127

not more persuasively—is in essence heroic. When a hero lacks this halo of suffering, we are instinctively repelled: he takes on the air of an executioner or tyrant.

> Leave the hero his heart! For what
> Will he become without it? A tyrant . . .[36]

Was it something to do with the heart (i.e., kindness) in that episode of "Napoleon among the plague-stricken" that so captivated Pushkin?[37] No, it was about something more than the heart: it was about the same thing as the episode in which Cleopatra sells herself. "And maybe a fateful game."[38] And maybe the hope of showing the heavens that there is such a person who does not consider himself above accepting the heavens' eternal challenge: is there such a person among you? (That is, one who rates himself highly enough so as to accept it). What kind of a person must this be? A free one. And what will come of this freedom? "We won't be—that's what will be"—as Pushkin wanted to have as an epigraph to "The Tales of Belkin."

Behind this seemingly suicidal instinct lies another meaning which I impose on no one: *Anima humana naturaliter christiana est.*[39] There is the hope of giving oneself up for the sake of an idea about oneself. There is the hope that the most loved part of your being, its sense and justifiability, will emerge in a pure form when it is freed not only from your "worst parts" but from *all* of you. And that it can only emerge in this way. And that your parting salute is dear to it, and that in all this is love. This is also enough for *naturaliter.* In the rarest of cases, however, poetry crosses beyond the bounds of this *naturaliter* that inhabits the depths of other motives. It would seem at times that the hour hand of art has reached the Fourth Eclogue[40]—and stopped there. When in its other state, we are used to calling it "no longer art," "more than art." (As someone initiated in the study of philology, I know that here we are speaking about one particular historical form of art. But having understood this does not mean we can overcome anything, we only think we can raise ourselves above history. Having studied, for example, the history of clothing and having learned that one's own dress is a particular historical form, you will not, however, be able to turn it into a *peplos* or pannier. Such a comparison is of course too superficial—but taking up any kind of canonical art would be a similar masquerade.[41] There are no rules banning anyone from dressing up, or less still from stylizing that same tunic, but the only thing that is genuinely ours is the internal dissatisfaction of the historical with its own form: the dissatisfaction of eternity's hostage with its captivity.)[42] Who laid down this dividing line between "art" and "no longer art," and can it be moved? You know Mikhail Shvartsman's answer to this: he says that moving this line will indeed see art returning to its source, that art knows no path other than the hieratic.[43] One must possess Shvartsman's gift in order to speak so conclusively. Evidently we feel that art, occupied as it is with the outermost peripheries of life, is becoming less and less necessary. But what if one day the need for any kind of art disappears? And what if next we see, not a hieratic art, but a silent feeling and experience that has no desire at all to be expressed?

To return to the hero: not only does he want to advance toward his own doom, this is what is wanted of him—or in him because this move must ultimately occur in someone. Lovers of "great lives" and bull fighting, the whole earth is tired of being in debt, tired of searching in the supreme powers for only a protector and the benefactor—and yet it does nothing else. And what is more, it comes up with the name "neurosis" for its free-floating anxiety and uses childhood trauma to explain it. Thus, by accepting the challenge of an undisguised anxiety of existence, the hero and the lyric poet (in as far as he is a hero) take on a challenge to "the simple life" and to "the people," (i.e., a challenge to the desire for the universe's heat death that is present in all our sweet routine), and a challenge to much that lies within them.

In any case, this decision is probably made easier by the fact that it is taken almost completely unconsciously. But can we call something that is unconscious or unfathomable even to ourselves a decision, i.e., a choice of will? I am certain that will operates much deeper than the realm of consciousness and memory (judging by dreams), and that it even plays a part in the constitution of the body. That each person—not of course by hair color or height, but in a barely definable way of the body—communicates certain information about him or herself, that is, about the choice of his or her will. It would be an inadmissible impertinence to attempt to read these signs: this is no matter of ours. This would be much worse than reading other people's letters, as I did at the start of these notes. By "will" I do not mean a negative trait that is self-restrictive and self-constraining, as is often meant, but rather—if we take the root of the word—something positive, closer to *volition*, deepest desire. Indeed it is not futile talking of a positive will beyond the bounds of consciousness: this type of will governs the external appearance of plants, twisting and straightening their stalks, turning their leaves and flowers in search of the sun's energy.

A year before hearing the poem about the wedding in black, I experienced, in comic form, the romantic conflict of "the poet and the crowd." This was preceded by an unusual event. I cannot describe it entirely seriously insofar as the level of sincerity of these notes is very relative—but, alas, no other way works for me. To all appearances it happened like this: two friends and I had set off to spend our winter holidays in a village near Uglich. There was a shortage of supplies in the village (New Year, 1965), and we took huge bags of food with us. Dizzy from carrying the bursting load onto the bus heading for the station, I started saying strange things: I told Olya and Lena that our seats in the train would be taken—there would be a mustachioed old man and a miserable old woman sitting in them, and we would ask them to give us our seats, but to no avail, and so would end up sitting on a wooden suitcase the whole way. This all happened. I had never come across wooden—i.e., plywood—suitcases before, and this was the most lucid part of my vision. Neither my friends nor I were particularly amazed, as this had happened to me before, and always at the least helpful moments. But this was a minor prelude to a larger fugue to be played out in an old blind man's *izba*.

On Christmas Eve we decided to tell our fortunes. We brought in a horse collar, prepared candles and other things. But the old woman next door told us such frightening stories about fortune-telling that by midnight we were too frightened to even step on the floor, let alone tell our fortunes. I was most taken aback by the hand mark left forever on a girl's cheek by her betrothed who had slapped her from a mirror. We moved the mirror back against the wall. I huddled up on the stove, frozen with fear. This is when the phenomenon occurred. I am unable to describe it very clearly as even then I did not understand what was happening. In any event, it had nothing to do with audible or visual hallucinations. It was something from within. The clearest image I can use to describe it is that the stove was at the center of the world, and this center was hurtling forward, or everything was hurtling past it on either side. It was by no means a feeling, but an event: it did not depend on whether I could sense it (just as an incident in the street does not depend on your perception of it). My life changed markedly following that night on January 7th. This says something about the power of that unfathomable occurrence, seeing as I treat all inner events, dreams, etc. (some of which would give even a more sober person cause to think) with great suspicion and I take no notice of them until I really have to. But I realized something here and I started, for the first time, to play truant from school. It was here that the parodic scene of "the poet and the crowd" took place, although I was not a poet and this new feeling, with its own "allowed" and "not allowed," had nothing to do with poetry. I was instructed to explain my truancy at a class meeting.

"I had a headache," I said evasively.

"So do we, but we come to school. Why is it that you are allowed to play truant and we aren't?" I pleaded with them not to insist, otherwise "you'll be offended." They kept on. So I explained: "Not everything in the world disappears. There is a non-disappearing thing. This thing can settle in someone, and then this person can do anything, including play truant."

"So this is what, your soul? Or God?" They laughed at such ideas with a sense of unreserved superiority. "I don't know," I said sincerely. "You can call it a pot if you like."[44] (My understanding of the soul was just the same as theirs.) They of course took my words precisely as I had feared, in a way I had not at all intended: that I was presenting myself, and not them, as a chosen person. And they decided to stop talking to me. For a long time after they teased me about the "pot." I would almost forget, when they would laugh: "Look, the pot has taken her over again!" This teasing did not affect me at all though, and the "pot" did not stop me from making up with everyone, studying well, going sledding on the Moscow River, and ceasing completely to experiment with this idea that "everything is allowed." Nor did it stop me from taking exams to study philology, although I wanted to study biology: I was too lazy to study botany and everything else.

Nor from writing poems that were still no good or about anything new, but were about something else entirely. This might not have been apparent to anyone trying to peer behind their shabby literary clothes. (Yes, once the "pot" had taken me over, my literary career was done for: up to this point some abominable poems of mine on the Komsomol and similarly banal themes had been published; it's dreadful thinking of them now.)

That challenging and fateful thing that I had been allowed to see—albeit through smoky glass—took a completely different form from the one in the verse about the bottle, which had so impressed me. It was something that seemed to come from the field of geometry, rather than a drama being acted out. And it was evoked each time by a geometrical image clothed in space: a road bound by straight lines or a circular room discernible within its cubic confines, or the verticals of a pine-tree park. Being a complete ignoramus in mathematics, I do not know whether there is such a thing as vectorial geometry—that is, with directions and points of gravity. Mine was vectorial.

＋

Maybe I was fatally mistaken and the contemplation of these figures gravitating, resisting, rotating, merging and receding along the perpendicular has nothing to do with the literary arts. As someone not particularly gifted at music or painting, I saw these pre-images manifested also here, and it seemed I could perhaps replicate them. I would not, of course, have been able to, and in any case I was frightened of those depths of wisdom, without even having tested them. But connecting words seems to be a simple business. Not surprisingly, there is no formal theory for it, unlike with music, and there is no academy, as there is for design and drawing. No musically ungifted person (in the strictest sense of the word "gift," i.e., being physically able to hear, sense rhythm, etc.) would attempt to compose a symphony. No person lacking a fast and accurate connection between the hand and eye would set about painting a still life. But in order to write a poem, the question of even the minimum amount of talent never arises. Everyone is talented enough to write, and those who publish their poems not much more so than others. Since the advent of free verse, not even an agility in finding assonances or a grasp of meter is required. Can we define the minimum *physical* talent a creator of verse requires? I believe Hans Christian Andersen did so in "The Galoshes of Fortune": the minimum talent required of a poet lies in memory. A particular kind, of course. A memory that allows the poet: not to miss the array of likenesses, repetitions, and contrasts that enter his own experience ("the image of the poet"); while looking at one object, to connect it to others that are alike ("metaphor," "simile"); to let not one tone of sound or development of line escape him ("tonal harmony"); not to see things bare, unclad in their centuries' old interpretations (poetic language, unlike prose, is less able to exist without "culture," "tradition," even if it only stands in opposition to what has gone before); not to hear words stripped of their roots and notional, aural, and stylistic contexts ("the singularity of poetic semantics").

Not to mention the memory of something else, a memory akin to foresight. For example, the false memory of pre-existence, of not being in the world for the first time, that is very close to a child's pensiveness. This is not a perception of the world as *déjà vu*, but of something that can be seen apart from the world and alongside it simultaneously—that can be seen without merging with its visible outlines. I do not like the idea of reincarnation, there is something bleak about it. It seems to me that here a sense of *incomplete* presence in the world merges with a sense of *not for the first time*, the former is taken for the latter—and then further unravels as a rational notion. It seems to me (can we actually know these things for sure?) that if someone actually remembered a pre-existence (with no play of imagination, which always has some cockerel or pharaoh at the ready), he would remember that he has not been and that this *not-being* would be incomparable with any *ceasing to be*. And he would probably not remember it as a sudden shock; instead, he would stand quietly on the podium of this once possible not-being—this discarded chance of not-being—and be attentive and grateful, because for him everything would be inwardly future . . .

And not to mention negative memory—of something that is not allowed, that is flat, used up—which is close to ethics.

Recollections that such a memory has at its disposal may be very dim, inexact, and ambiguous. The main thing is that they must be utterly real, irrespective of their quality—real, for example, like the cold outside, a cold from which there is no shelter. In a word, a memory of this kind can withstand the "soundless ether" of Shvarts's poem cited earlier. The poet, as in "The Galoshes of Fortune," should not remember, but recall:

> The distance, my friends, between remembering
> And recalling is as far as from Luga
> To the land of the satin Bauta.[45]

(This is Akhmatova: you can hear how she recalled both Luga and a Bauta on the spot). The champion of poetic memory is undoubtedly Dante. One Italian language textbook included an anecdote about Dante's memory: "One day a stranger approached Dante in the square and asked, 'What's the most delicious thing in the world?' Dante gave his answer: 'An egg.' A year passed. The stranger approached Dante, who was wandering through noisy streets, and asked, 'With what?' 'Salt,' Dante replied.")[46]

This is the kind of shape the great poet kept himself in. He is racing against oblivion, disappearance, lack of attention, and ultimately against decomposition. This "salt" fascinates me more than Boccacio's tale of how Dante was able to reproduce from memory a long theological dispute on a free theme. If this is true, if it is with "salt," then it means that time, to a certain extent, no longer exists.

Lyric composition, like musical composition, transforms time, offering an alternative to the flow of things that seek to supersede one another: it offers the figure of their co-presence, where the existence of each thing is reproduced in the other. There is something of paradise in the ideal poem. Great works of poetry are utterly bold in taking time in all its external ruin, they are never miserly, saving the "best places" from extinction, and in the most real way they embrace this ruin of flux with something that is unforgettable, ineradicable. Weighing down on nineteenth-century Russian lyric poetry is the threat of real duration, linearity, narrativity (but at the same time, it is precisely this non-transformed physical continuance, this headlong style of composition, that was the charm of the Nekrasov construction!). Looming over "new" Russian lyric poetry is another danger: an absolute break with temporal continuity and the purposefulness of language, when the whole resembles a fan of versions (particularly with Mandelstam).

We can see from Pushkin's drafts how a memory of this type struggled with "immediate feeling" and with sense destined for expression.

These—feeling and sense—turned out to be prosaic. Leo Tolstoy, having replaced the epithet "sad" in the last line of "Memories":

> But I do not wipe away the sad lines
> *No strok pechal'nykh ne smyvaiu*[47]

with "shameful" (*postydnykh*), showed that he did not feel how much *memory* there was in the original, more restrained adjective chosen by Pushkin.

I keep digressing and digress I will a little further—to an analysis of Tolstoy's correction. The rationale for the phonetic weakening of the line is as follows: the monotonous *a* of the final words has disappeared (*pechál'nykh ne smyváiu*), which was set against the contrasting vocalism of the rhyming line (*ia trepeshchú i proklináiu*, I tremble and curse)—a monotonous mournful cry on the *a* after outbursts akin to the tearing of clothes. Gone is the strangeness of the crystalline yet soft consonance of *pechal'nykh* (sad): *postydnykh* (shameful) duplicates the former alliteration—but what is lacking, sorely lacking, in it is an "r": for total duplication it would need to be *prestupnykh* (criminal), which Tolstoy decided against. From the lexico-semantic point of view, *prestupnykh* would have maintained the force of words such as *s otvrashcheniem* (with disgust) and *trepeshchu* (I tremble). Putting "shameful" after them is like putting "slap" in the place of "thrash." The decision to remove *pechal'nykh* (sad) is a breach not only of the flow of Pushkin's poem but the flow of Pushkin's whole lexicon in which *pechal'nyi*, like *zhivoi* (alive), has an unusual range of meaning. *Pechal'nyi*, with its sound and semantic vitality, is associated with Pushkin's name (as some melodic phrases are with Chopin's name and some color preferences with Rembrandt's name) to such an extent that when saying "creative sadness" or "my sadness is heavy"[48] the later poet casts the reflected light of Pushkinism over his or her verse. But the main alteration is this: in the place of a generalizing and contrasting adjective, Tolstoy inserts one that has a weakening and duplicating effect.

It is difficult to give a fine poem an ending that is stronger than its beginning. Only an unexpected final movement that transcends its limits can relieve this tension. Which is what the word *pechal'nykh*— the final judgment on those "lines"—does. And what does it do exactly? It communicates a new point of view on the author's life: a chronicler's point of view.[49] To call that which is the object of the cruelest remorse "sad" means to look at it from a "marvelous distance" or from a "marvelous approach," and not from the demands of the actual moment. There is a certain point of view from which both the question torturing Ivan Karamazov, and Ivan himself, who poses it, are not "tormenting" but "sad." And this, if you like, is in a certain sense "worse," not "easier": it suggests the intrusion of something like death. It is perhaps apparent from this description that prosaism consists of the egoistic use of a word and of literary composition written to "express someone's feelings and thoughts" (even the best). It lies in a predetermined move of language that leaves no room for a miraculous conclusion; in the disharmony of composition that is sure to accompany it; and, finally, in the shallow, familiar sense of the single word. But in our case we have learned something new about the word "sad" (as well as about remorse, which would also seem only too familiar when described using Tolstoy's "strong" epithet).

Prosaism is, I believe, the absence of that kind of memory, which, incidentally, I do not know what to call (no matter whether it consists of "uncultured" words and meanings or, conversely, of poetic phrases that have been devalued). Thus, memory allows the poet to become more than himself, to become a "momentary character creating these lines," as Paul Valéry said, or the person "such as eternity finally makes him," as Stéphane Mallarmé said of Edgar Allan Poe. The very commitments to sound by which poets abided until recently require the favor of Mnemosyne. Strictly speaking, the only satisfactory way to know poetry is to know it by heart. The poet must tremble at the thought of writing something that he knows to be *memorabile*. And not burden this "ideal," fictitious, or universal memory with detestable nonsense or trivialities. Is it possible to develop a poetic memory as with music or drawing skills? I would not know how. Perhaps by one's way of life. In any case, special attempts at memorizing will be of no help here. As happens in Andersen's tale, the poet unwittingly recalls that which he unwittingly memorized. It would seem to him that certain things recall themselves to mind. Otherwise they would not be able to appear in a new, changed, and changing form—as with everything that is committed to memory with a marksman's instinct to "use" it later. And a hundred times blessed is the poet whose unconscious, restless, and eager memory steps in not at the moments that take his fancy, apparent only to him, but at the moments of reality, history, and language that are truly central and rich in meaning. A lyrical memory such as this is bestowed by the will of heaven and, doubtless, is preserved through a strength of mind—and perhaps of conscience too.

◆

Now, with the help of Andersen, I return to those geometrical images long since abandoned. He did more than define the typical poet, *poeta communis*. One such image that was evoked by his work and became an early favorite of mine was, in Derzhavin's words:

> . . . a certain heavy sphere
> Hanging by a thin little thread.[50]

The image is of a closed house standing alit in the northern wind and rain, a wintry garden or window boxes hanging over a city street, happiness in a peapod.

A sense of the world as closed, its seeming coziness—warmed and lit up—gave me an almost unbearable surge of joy when I was fifteen or sixteen. All around it was everything else: pitch dark, immense, incommensurate. I could not, and did not try to, imagine what this *everything else* was like; its business was to be unimaginable. But then it was easy to imagine the closed spherical world: lit from the inside, half-lit from below, as though from an open stove or fireplace; it was lit and instantly aglow like the figures in a Rembrandt. The most important thing was not the world as such, but its encounter with *everything else*. A visitor from this *everything else* could not be expected to be anything other than pernicious: the Naughty Boy or shivering Cupid. In Andersen's version I did not understand that the arrow was deadly in a different way: here he was talking about love.[51] I thought that this Naughty Boy was a simple murderer, an innocent, because not he, but his nature—he was part of the bad weather beyond the window—was to blame. But it was not so much a question of the boy here, but the owner of the spherical house: he was aware of everything, perhaps omniscient and clairvoyant. And the fact that he could let in a visitor, knowing or guessing how it would all end, seemed to me a miracle. And so this miracle, but not kindness as such (I never liked kindness, particularly in my youth), was more precious than a happy ending and more precious than anything else. Only Andersen, it seems, could combine a miracle with what is a "bad" ending according to the rules of fairytales (especially in

"The Little Match Girl"). This, in short, is the prelude to a "Danish Tale"[52] in the inclement autumnal Moscow Region.

I don't usually remember the moment in time when I composed a particular poem, often not even the year, but I do remember the places very clearly. Because each poem is to some extent a portrait of a place. The portrait is barely discernible, remaining far beyond the threshold of the immediate content of the poem. There are only a few of these places, and I will try to describe them—although there is nothing more boring in any art form than landscape. With or without allegories, in a novel or in descriptive music, in lyric poetry and naturalistic painting, all landscapes essentially consist of epithets, and they torment me as evidence of human mediocrity: "Light bluish shadows lay across the reddish grass," for example . . . Pah!

> Shatter yourself like a warped mirror
> before which they stood: and it
> remained empty.[53]

How can we do without borrowings: *peizash, landshaft?* Maybe the word *okrestnost'* (surroundings) will do.[54]

So then, the surroundings of the village of Mashutino, halfway between the Holy Trinity-St. Sergius Lavra and Aleksandrov,[55] was my father's birthplace. There are no surroundings without a guardian spirit. And each *genius loci* loves its own style and themes. Mashutino is the setting for the "Legends," children's poems about Saint Aleksei,[56] and other such poems. The spirit of this place has a love for unending melancholy, similar to the love found in Rilke's "Book of Hours": *Sehnsucht.* Even joy in Mashutino is melancholic and the people say: "if we must die, let it be with music." It is a flat and barren place where the wind howls, and there are no wide rivers or high banks, no forests or lakes. It would seem that History has not been there (although the historical site of Deulino is not far),[57] and that everything has always been slipping into a drunken or drowsy oblivion. (In actual fact, judging from stories, it had been a bustling and merry place, the forest was well cared for and there were weirs on the streams.) No other place would have suited more being called a "God forsaken place." Mashutino, it seemed to me, was like a boat left adrift on an ocean of land.

Another place is Valentinovka, the dacha. The spirit of this place was also the spirit of late spring and early summer. A few cherry trees behind the house made up the huge garden, a heavenly garden. And the few pine trees in front of the house were a grove of ship masts and spoke only of height. Because of the trees' height everything at Valentinovka happened deep down below, on a bed of floating sea and rushing leaves. Here the bond to the sky was much looser: being so far away little of it was visible, fir cones would fall down from it, and your attention—which had only to follow the movement of the tree trunks—climbed up to it easily. The immense open sky of Mashutino was out of reach, it was the subject and the cause of the melancholy there. Here in Valentinovka the dampness, unsteadiness, and creaking was quite musical.

And Saltykova was the place, later on, of "Tristan and Isolde" and the "Stanzas"[58]—our acquaintances had a dacha here. The crystal heart of winter would arrive at Saltykova; it was especially limpid there because the village was broken up into straight streets, as in Leningrad. For me this point in winter always provided an inexhaustible source of lyrical themes, and I was later surprised to learn that winter was also T. S. Eliot's favorite ("The Four Quartets"—and its ending, with the knot of a rose, is suspiciously similar to my "Elegy on a Rose." I have not read his "Journey of the Magi," but I fear I will discover there my own "Journey of the Magi").

But the center of all the places, the stolen cradle, is Perovo Pole, which at that time was part of the Moscow Region. It is now a housing development. The windowless (despite there being thousands of windows) concrete speaks of the end of the world or perhaps the start of a new civilization. But this used to be a place of petty bourgeois life with rowan and silver fir bark between the double window frames, woodworm patterns, valances on the beds, pails in the hay, and wild cucumbers on the fence. A house ruled over this place: in the house was a stove, by the stove my grandmother. God willing, I will write about her one day. I have never met a more Christian person; it seems it is more unusual to meet a true Christian than a genius in this world. Perovo Pole reminded me, as a whole, of a deep carved cradle, the scoop of folded palms, a basket of unlit coal.[59]

Azarovka, where I wrote almost everything, came later, but I am not going to speak of it here.[60]

I do not need to revisit these places. I can see them without closing my eyes. And I not only see the things I remember, but can also sometimes examine or find a new knot in the floorboard at Perovo Pole, or a stand of bushes at Mashutino. These are probably gifts from the spirits of those places. Like everything in the world (even if they conceal it from themselves), they want to have their say, and are pleased if a listener comes their way. For each thing, as I see it, has been made for more attention than it is usually given, but it has long since become used to the way things are and will not ask for more: yet how it will smile if someone suddenly breaks the natural order of things to fall silent and listen! Sometimes something like ripples can be seen over newly plowed earth: this is the pull of objects to be loved, their right to be noticed, their unassauged desire to give. Tears simply flow at this almost visible haze, and the word "poor," the one word for everything, resounds in my thoughts. In what way are they *poor*, you might ask? Because they are here. All that remains is to lie around on the earth before the terrible wonder of unbidden universal humility.

While waxing sentimental like Radishchev[61] I have forgotten to mention my hometown. But I remember little about Moscow and have not been able to write there for a long time. The only thing I like about the whole of Moscow is a certain drowsiness one falls into by lamplight when someone reads. I do not mean to find fault with the city in favor of village peace and quiet: there can be hustle and bustle and noise anywhere at all, and creative dreams are more vivid[62] in the places of their choosing.

I cannot put down all there is to say about surroundings and places. Besides geographical features, there are things such as *forest, steppe, hill, embankment, attic, corridor*—and many other modes of thought. I once dreamed of crystal spears and they were called *mountains* (the Urals at that), I dreamed of a *corridor* that was a stretch of steppe hills with rivers disappearing under ground and reappearing. Apart from describing physical objects, the names for various types of landscape signify something else as well: certain constant images. As if they were all various folds lying within the same depth, the last, final depth. A sense of the end can, after all, just as easily latch onto the image of a *steppe, forest, sea,* or *corridor*.

Apart from places, birds and berries had a strong presence in my first poems. I will keep the birds to myself but will tell you about the berries. One autumn we visited Pasternak's grave. There was a wild rose bearing dark hips that looked black in the dark and rain. I ate my fill of them and felt quite strange. Then I forgot all about it. And then in the winter the beginnings of "The Wild Rose" came to me out of the blue:

My soul has nurtured a wild rose—[63]

I did not know what this could mean. Another time, we ate a lot of wild strawberries growing in an untended graveyard in the Onega region, also dark and sickeningly sweet, too much like blood. Later, when I read back a poem I had just written, also a few months on:

The flow of trees by the roadside
reddens. Juice so clear in the wormwood,
greenish in the tender viper,
turned crimson in my veins.
And near is the earth's peaty blood—

I could taste Onega there once more.

My attempts to forge connections between poems and events are of course pointless: I doubt whether we can say what is really connected to what; what caused the cloud swirling wordlessly in my mind to burst—a cloud that is not really connected to any cause. Besides words, besides rhythm, besides meaning, what else is there? What is it that torments us, contracting and expanding, growing near and far like a dry cloud of dust, with a kind of supersonic whistling? Without what does life seem emptier than empty? The only thing I can call it is: "something new." In order to explain what meaning I attach to this "something new" (because what meaning is not attached to it?),

I shall permit myself a brief account of one of the "Considerations of the Holy Stigmata" (from the "Little Flowers" of Saint Francis of Assisi). Saint Francis is often called a "poet of faith"—as others are called knights, warriors and laborers of faith—and not only because the Graces and Mirth whirl round his words ushering in every one of the poet's creations. He reveals an ideal and unfathomable model of poetic work, one that is taken up from the earth into the heavens, where there is no freedom without devotion and no awe without freedom. Meekness blazes there like an all-consuming fire and every inward thing is manifest in a delightful form. St. Francis told his "brother lamb" that he had been conversing with a heavenly guest, who said:

> "Francis, bring me an offering."
> "But I have nothing my Lord."
> "Search in thy bosom (*nel grembo*)."

And he searched and found a golden ball. He was asked a second and third time—and for a second and third time he found and offered up a golden ball. He was then told that these three balls signified three virtues that, unbeknown to him, he possessed.

Since he had nothing concealed in his "bosom," he would not have been able to find anything less than the miraculous there: and what is more miraculous than a golden ball? This is what I believe is the only new thing.

Poetic meaning must be new in this way. It is wrong to think that poetry concentrates, encapsulates, or heightens meaning that already exists without it, in "reality." It operates from the other side:

And over the raging sea
It pours a soothing balm.[64]

Meaning such as this does not exist in the world, but there is a need for it in the world: precisely because it is not there, because there is nothing to find in one's bosom and offer up. The world is given; meaning is bestowed. Poetry does not take its balm from the raging sea as if it were the "essence" of this sea, but offers its balm *to* the sea: like something that is present there only for the want of it, as an object of longing, a plea. What is the sea longing and raging for? However absurd and pretentious it might sound—for absolute existence. For the sting of non-existence to be plucked out—together with the pain of movement and indeed everything, everything that seeks to devour and displace everything else. It longs for that which is not given, but can only be bestowed.

It seems to me that this is also how things stand for the "voices of the spirit of the people," which do not so much epitomize and nobly reproduce this national spirit as provide an answer to its longing. Pushkin expresses that which is Russian—but in the sense that he is bestowed to it (and not to any other), that it is *this* "raging sea" he pours his soothing balm over. In this way, he also "expresses" a Russian language that did not exist before.

Why speak of this endlessly outdated idea, "the spirit of the people"? Because I want to move away, anywhere, from the story I have undertaken to tell. It is approaching an unpleasant moment. In "Safe Conduct," Pasternak explains wonderfully that we lag behind life when telling the truth: life, at that moment, is already in a different place from the truth we tell about it. He lived in fast-moving times, while ours grow menacingly stagnant. All the same, even in a lull such as this, it is best to tell lies in advance. I am about to touch on the state of being in love, and I have already undertaken to report on the events surrounding my first poems, so I had better return to my last digression and tell you just what it was that Pushkin bestowed to the "spirit of the people"—just as Peter bestowed his fleet to the State. This riddle was solved by Fyodor Tiutchev, but I do not feel his solution is fully appreciated:

> And you, like first love,
> Russia's heart will not forget![65]

We underestimate this remarkable definition because of our weak grasp of its syntax. It does not say that Pushkin was the first beloved poet, an object of first love. Look closer: it explicitly says that he was this first love, the state of love; he was that *which* loves. Do you recall Tatiana's conversation with her nurse about love?[66] This was, to a certain extent, how Russia used to love before Pushkin, like the nurse. None of these qualities—". . . artless, and without concealing, / her love obeys the laws of feeling, / that she's so trustful, and imbued / by heaven with such an unsubdued / imagination, with such reason, / such stubborn brain, and vivid will, / and heart so tender, it can still / burst to a fiery blaze in season?"[67]—of Pushkinian love had yet been seen. At least no one had ever spoken of it. They would talk of a terrible passion more like an illness that could be brought on by a love spell and that consumed Frol Skobeev;[68] and about the tenderness of Peter and Fevronia[69] and of spiritual poetry;[70] about marital fidelity and respect, and lastly, "the art of tender passion" from the times of the red heels.[71] But this:

> Like Desdemona choosing
> An idol for her heart,[72]

was set as an example by Pushkin. What should we call this kind of free choice? Somewhere far behind it is the strange enamorment of the Poor Knight.[73] Pushkin's Desdemona is only an example: I stress ten times over that it is not a question of a "new attitude to women"—it is a "new attitude to life" and above all to art. Pushkin's readers came to see the objects of his inspiration as objects *for their hearts*, one of the most important objects being beauty—and it was beauty of a new kind.

Of course Pushkin alone cannot occupy all the space that his name does. We have attributed labors and discoveries that occurred both before and after Pushkin to this name, and used it to overshadow them, transforming him from a poet into a latter-day Orpheus. What is more, his name signifies something, which though not altogether formless, is hard to define. In all manner of places where we experience the true delight of art, something takes shape in the mind akin to what is elsewhere known as "Pushkin": the first poet for love, the first poet of love, first love, as the poet of the last love said of him.[74]

I am not, believe me, talking of the official Pushkin or Pushkin as hero and teacher, serious like Lermontov or, worse, Bulgarin.[75] It is bad to burden Pushkin with such seriousness and doing the exact opposite is no better. With all his ironic and non-ironic stylization, Pushkin is perhaps the sincerest of all our poets (melodramatic sincerity like Esenin's is quite a different matter). Pushkin's irony concerns the "poet-reader" relationship: such irony is a courtesy among one's own, where dreary elucidation and pathos are unbecoming, and it is not so much an arrogant form of restraint as a way to protect this "rubbish" (as Charsky spoke of inspiration) from outsiders: far hence be souls profane![76] In his relations with the Muse, Pushkin is trusting and respectful like few others. And, like almost no other, he *serves* poetic suggestion, and because of this, his words cannot carry the full weight of those edifying meanings that many would like to see in them and reveal to others.[77] Such meanings are present among those who are rhetorical, even if only in the best sense of this word. At the heart of concrete meaning in Pushkin's work is its non-insistence (often called "ambivalence"), less when taken alone, than when compared to something else: to Poetry—the comforter angel.[78] Indeed inspiration is the underlying theme of his most diverse and "problematic" work, and so does it matter where it can be found?

> In a splendid hall, a chic theater box,
> Or in a nomad's *kibitka*?[79]

This is why Pushkin was able to borrow almost all his material from authors writing in other languages: for here the instruments are ready-made, created by others, leaving all the more time to play undistracted without having to invent them. If Pushkin has a lesson to share, it is a lesson in inspiration, which reveals itself to us as life and as an act of grace, but above all as life.

My likening of Pushkin's borrowed material (plots, themes, even similes and lines) to music that is played on a ready-made instrument is only approximate. It is rather an improvisation on a given theme. We note, however, that with Pushkin any such theme must not be too widely known, or recognizable: not because he will be "accused of plagiarism,"[80] but because too obvious a theme attracts much attention and gives the careless reader license to turn a deaf ear to everything else that remains, the most important thing. The theme should be as neutral, as prosaic, as possible: an ever-present theme or something completely random, because without just that piece of "prose," of "material," you cannot, unfortunately, construct art (unfortunately or fortunately, that is). And Pushkin, with his impatience, his "all at once," and with his "not yet—but already,"[81] no doubt wishes to linger as little as possible in the anteroom of "ideas," "plots," or "strong images." We have the simple, promising things that are already to hand and then—to work. "And light-footed rhymes come racing towards them."[82]

There are poets of the opposite constitution, the most obvious of them being Khlebnikov (my second favorite Russian poet, by the way): their source of inspiration seems to be marvelously rich, generating "ideas" or "images" with natural ease. Poets similarly minded to Khlebnikov are most often called genius: their genius is perceived as astounding originality, as discovery. Pushkin is perhaps not a genius in this sense; he is weak at inventing new concrete meanings and original scenes; he does not possess an inherent strangeness of gaze, i.e., some not altogether normal point of view. And I will love Pushkin no less if I learn that all of his material is borrowed, like one of his loveliest images, taken from Shakespeare's *Cleopatra*:

> . . . I mingle
> Tears with a smile, like April[83]

Whoever guesses where inspiration is leading will realize that no image is anything more than a pretext:

> from paper see it rise—
> a spire to empty skies.[84]

What are these *empty skies* toward which it is only possible to rise by giving the eye a near or far-off point, some scenery, a depth—some kind of *other* thing? I fear that admirers of fullness and richness, intensity and brightness in art will not know what is at stake here. In fact no one can know, but some can hazard a guess. When borrowing material, Pushkin elevates it from being a mathematical equation to an algebraic formula. He makes the grounds, the pretext, for inspiration clearer, which arises thanks to, and in spite of, that pretext: like pictorial depth, which is created thanks to the curtain and foreground, and in spite of them. Deep inspiration, like deep life and deep sleep, deals with a place that has no images, no ideas, nothing at all. A place where everything is *whole*. And that same scenery, spire, pretext, or ground, from behind which we come to recognize such a total absence, makes it clear: everything *is made whole again, healed*. I do not mean to say that Khlebnikov or any like-minded "discoverer" poet cannot enter this domain. They enter it when their readers become poets at every given pretext or prompt:

in these days of the golden ball[85]

and we instantly construct that same "airy colossus"[86] (only without words) that Pushkin constructs—using words—in an image borrowed from Horace. I am not comparing these two constitutions so as to demean one in favor of the other. People here believe that comparisons can only be used for this.

Of all the idiotic ideas that can enter the head of a fifteen year old, I had the idea that poets received all their best poems from Pushkin, and that these waves emanated from his statue.[87] I promised to bring him a basket of flowers but still, to this day, have not done so because there was a condition: "when I'm a poet" (in particular "when I'm published"). Khlebnikov is typically called "a poet's poet," but there is another poet's poet—Pushkin:

And I will be praised in the moonlit world
As long as one bard remains alive.[88]

Maybe all the others are partly the same (even from Bunin we have: "To future poets whom I know not, God will leave a secret—the memory of me").[89] Esteemed shadows and souls who remain nameless to us still want something from the living (I continue to insist on the sweet delusions of a fifteen year old): they are still waiting for their secret hopes to be fulfilled, and perhaps their impatience spurs on our lazy blood, forces us to take an oath and try to listen to that which cannot be heard.

✦

I turn now to living poets, our literature's lost generation. I have known them since my school years when we studied together at the Palace of Pioneers[90] literature workshop. From seeing this children's version I can imagine what the Union of Writers was like with its field trips, commissions, etc. There were gifted poets there, much more gifted than I. I greatly pity our generation, which promised to produce nothing less than "a wave of Evtushenkos,"[91] but it suffered a more barren and much harder fate. Public performances of "young geniuses" (this is what those a year or two older called themselves) came to an end when SMOG was dissolved.[92] At that time it was a case of everyone for him or herself. Things in Leningrad turned out better than in Moscow, where our literary life was buried alive just as it was getting started. I am not sure how far I can compare this torture with the tragedy of the older generation: no blood was shed, but it was creativity that was destroyed. Once I entered university, I lost contact with living poets, and gave no more thought to literary life. I wanted to study, and, even more, wander through the city and suburbs with N.N.

By this time I had also stopped going to see Mikhail Grigorievich Erokhin, my music teacher. He had not been able to teach me to play the piano, but this was through no fault of his own: I had neither the ability to work hard at music nor to compose music. But he taught me something else. He explained pieces of music to me in terms of canvases. He would ask me to play certain pieces like a particular kind of landscape or poem—and this was not merely talk about art: he was himself a visitor from those parts. He was interested in my banal verse and saw something in it. Talking about one such monstrosity he mentioned Rilke, who for many years became "poetry itself" for me. "If I were your mother," said Mikhail Grigorievich, "this poem would scare me. Journals are all full of poems like it, but for a writer of thirteen, and besides, there's something . . . something here about how man is on a path of no return . . . a path that

> he who departed is still wandering
> or has long since perished on the way.[93]

That's Rilke. Do you know this poet? It's a translation, of course . . ."

I did not know, but was transfixed. I learned that there are some things alongside which life is no different from death. The one who died had, all the same, departed, and his departure was living, and he is, in some way, still wandering. And this Rilkean longing, which in the *Book of Hours* "reaches God," almost killed me with its truth that cannot be at home and has no place to go to—and was then forgotten for another five years. In the end, Mikhail Grigorievich gradually brought me around to music. And after giving up lessons I began to love it painfully, in a way I have not loved it since. I called my poems ballads, not meaning the literary genre but the ballads of Chopin, which for me were the most moving expressions of art. Poetry seemed peripheral to me (and the plastic arts were still further from the center). It was like a retelling in one's own words of some strange news—pernicious or salvatory, I know not—or like the urgent call to do something like that which Tolstoy describes in "The Kreutzer Sonata" through the hatred of an acutely musical person. A bitter enemy of Eros, it was only in the erotic that he found a way to satisfy the demands of music. Or more so in the ruin of the central character in "The Living Corpse."[94] Having now lost my sensitivity to the language of music, instead of urgent calls, I find there consequences. The point is that something emerges in "life," philosophy, poetry, and painting as the *consequence* of everything that has happened and that has already moved beyond its own reality, beyond even its "content": a certain intellectual and sensory sum total, an "indiscernible residue." But this is not the point either: those diverse "residues" are the actual material of music. It is no surprise that musicians often love the stilted splendor of poetry: they make use of ready-made emotional effects that are not legitimate in the verbal art of composition. I do not wish to offend musicians; poets also love the already present semantic sum total to be found in painting—besides, who knows what anyone likes . . .

Had I not been able to attune myself to music I would never have earned the trust of N.N., whose words for me were like those of an oracle. For him musicality was an ideology: "The man that hath no music in himself . . . Let no such man be trusted."[95] Let me describe for you the ideology that so captured me. It was a longing for an "elsewhere," not the elsewhere that gently glows like firelight by the Old Poet, or the oil lamp at my grandmother's house, and appears to lie at the very core of our present "here": but for a beautiful lavender-white elsewhere, external and faraway, which flares and fades, after which everything becomes especially dark and all that is "here" torments you and drives you far away. And now I know where. "That faint purple-gray halo that I saw once before."[96] (This contrasting image of light and dark calls to mind one of Mikhail Grigorievich's lessons in which he illuminated a Bach prelude that I had found boring: an old man enters his empty quarters and lights a candle, a corridor lit up behind him unfolds its dimensions; before him is a darkness that can only be sensed, invisible and unfathomable to the eye). Intertwined into this comet-like flame was everything that is usually intertwined there: Dostoevsky, Nietzsche, the death of Isolde, some extracts from the mystics, Baudelaire and, by a strange irony, Thomas Mann wryly contemplating this whole array (as a rule Thomas Mann and in particular his Leverkühn had the same effect on my peers as Goethe once had with his Werther;[97] I have encountered more than one imitator of this hero). Arguments between my new idol and my old one—the poet and my mentor in poetry V. Lapin[98]—were absurdly reminiscent of the quarrels between Nafta and Settembrini.[99] Unlike the hero of *The Magic Mountain*, I had no sympathy for "daytime humanism": anything that could not transcend itself—if not toward purity and sublimity, then at least toward depth and strangeness—bored me. The depth and strangeness of the world by daylight is more difficult to understand than the fathomless vaults of the Queen of the Night.[100]

> *Tief ist die Nacht, tief ist die Nacht.*
> *Und tiefer als der Tag gedacht.*[101]

Also intertwined here were befitting fragments from completely unbefitting poets: "With death we feasted well" and "With burning splinter I enter" from Mandelstam, and "All, all that bodes of death," and the like from Pushkin.[102] And by no means last were Socrates' speeches from his "Apology," "The Banquet," and "Phaedrus." I will not list everything, but we called this wild love potion—you will gasp—a Christian sense of life. Suffering was considered to be the noblest of values, and the noblest feat of belief was to leap into the abyss. The damned took their place at the top of the human hierarchy, while kind and decent people were at the very bottom in the Dantesque pit for the worthless. The prodigal son's model brother seemed to be a negative character, while the prodigal son was a hero and model, as if this parable were not about miraculous mercy and hope, but the need to squander everything to start with.

Alas, even today in the Tillichian "abyss and ground"[103] it is easier for me to understand the "abyss," but my mind of course has no need for the bare abyss. The "damned" have lost much of their sheen for me today, which is, in particular, thanks to an exemplary prodigal son— the author and hero of *Moscow-Petushki*.[104] But that is another story. N.N. explained Christianity to me in terms of pain and ill health, both inherent to the soul. (Ill health and all forms of wretchedness were just as much in fashion at that time as health is today: illness was seen as a way out of a blocked non-creative state, whereas today it is a hindrance to Yogic perfection.) He was not overly enlightened; I was still more ignorant, but he was inspirational and I fervently believed that I had to plunge my soul into chaos so that a star would shine forth from it. If this is indeed the way to the stars, it is a very indirect one. Once on this path you will be lucky if you don't lose sight of the goal (you surely will) and also of that which the prodigal son did not forget: his last hope.

But my head was not filled with star-spawning chaos alone. There was also, for example, Tynianov's *Problem of Poetic Language*.

This book spurred me on no less than *Beyond Good and Evil*. For me it meant: "Beyond the Dictionary." After reading it, none of our poets seemed to have reached anywhere near that level of freedom promised by the "resultant of two series: the syntactic and the rhythmic."[105] I was, of course, mistaken here as well; some possibilities exist only so they are not used. Especially in art, which for centuries has been content with a very limited range of freedom of form. It seemed to me that Tynianov was describing not poetry that already existed, but the poetry of the future. In a word, you can distance yourself in any direction and as far as you like from the dictionary—to the oscillating signs of meaning, to the non-differentiated flickering of sense. While all disarticulation and expression of sense seemed to me false, impudent and simplistic, worse than theft.[106] Naturally, the falsest of all were aphorisms.

As I near the end of the "circumstances," I shall also briefly recall the atmosphere of those years, the end of the Thaw—although here I am a poor chronicler. We grew up surrounded by adults who delighted in their unexpected freedom like children, their new right not to lie, not to be afraid, and not to be suspicious. The sexual revolution had not yet happened, nor had the economic reforms; the purified ideals that the socialist revolution had borrowed from the rosewater of Christianity still sparkled.[107] All the more so, as in order to purify these ideals, injustices were being eliminated before our very eyes, scoundrels were being exposed and everyone was "telling the truth" at their own risk and peril. The risk and peril was, of course, not so great, because this truth did not fully confront the authorities and was encouraged by them. But this "conscience-led life" did promote general goodwill, ease, hospitableness, and enjoyment. Teachers, who were tired of years of casting aspersions (voluntary or enforced) on one another, their subjects, predecessors and colleagues abroad, now visibly unwound before their jubilant pupils. Professor A. would begin a lecture thus: "I congratulate you dear colleagues! The last national injustice has been eliminated: the Crimean Tatars have been allowed to return to the Crimea." What would he say today? Politics, by the way, was simply the backdrop to our interests, inasmuch as these interests could not have arisen earlier for reasons that were themselves political. For example, general linguistics: "Now that we know that descriptive linguistics is not a weapon of imperialism . . ."[108] The last injustice. There will be no more. There will be a descriptive, and even generative linguistics. There will be genetics, talents will create freely—like Voznesensky: "Play, Columbus!"[109] At that time everyone, as you will remember, loved poems, whatever they could manage, but one more bold deed was expected of the poetic form itself. People copied out poems just as they copy out horoscopes, diets and massages today. And the "truth" that they were now waiting for was best expressed in dense detailed prose—the more naturalistic the better. I did not notice when these things started to change because I was slowly losing my mind.

At the end of my first year at university I had a serious accident on a racing bicycle; miraculously it was not fatal. After this I lost all interest in "ordinary life"—I did not know what to do with it. I was living at Seliger[110] and would go for long walks in the forest there. For a long time, I had been haunted by a line from the Psalms, "the waters are come in unto my soul" and by a "geometrical form": two intercepting lines of movement, one stronger than the other, resulting in a pull toward the strongest. The forests at Seliger are neglected and dense, everything is heavy with the nearby marshland; fungus, moss and bracken are everywhere, and all around are places that could be inhabited by the One-Eyed Likho, day-demons, wood sprites and other half-men half-beasts from Slavic folk tales.[111] The image of the two opposing currents that had been tormenting me attached itself to this half-beast creature and, like a barely lit flame, a poem came to me. I have only ever understood one way of composing: toward a crescendo. Perception itself, as I see it, requires a heightened intensity of sense, sound and structuring, and does not abate even when reaching a pitch so high that cannot be surpassed. I perceived stability as a sliding down. So, sitting on a tree I drew this "Poem" out to a crescendo, and in the middle came the direct speech—which frightened me—of a hero talking and acting independently. And later when a "hero's" declaration suddenly (I swear that this is sudden—most of all for me; it is not a preconceived device) interrupts a narrative, this always means for me that we are now at the epicenter of the original image: everything is speaking on its own. This hero is not a front; often he is completely unlike me, and he is also unlike whatever it is I want to say. He says things that I would not choose to say or want to hear. The phonetic crescendo of the "Poem" led to a deliberately monotonous reverberation at the end—to an almost, or even very, bland alliteration and assonance of "u," "du," and "no." N.N. did not approve of this insistent alliteration. But I left it unchanged.

After the "Poem" yet more romantic madness rapidly fermented into the clinical kind and it all ended the natural way: with a suicide attempt. It is very unpleasant remembering this, but what can you do.

I had no immediate reasons to want to do this and I probably lamented the fact that there were none. But then there was little I was able to grasp, although I was passing my exams with distinction.

I pleaded with my mother to take me to Kislovodsk for the winter holidays because there was one way I wanted to do it: by jumping off a mountain. You think I was imitating Sappho, for example? No such thing. Before doing it I wanted to have a look at the mountains, which I had never seen before. And so I saw them, got up to a high viewing platform and neared the edge. The sun was high, the mountains peopleless. I came round when the sun was setting. And I forgot what I was there for. I thought only that I had better make my way down into the town before dark. Last year's grass was burning on the slopes. I ran into the hotel with scorched clothes. My mother was in bed having a heart seizure: she had understood everything. The next day we flew to Moscow and a few days later I found myself in a noisy ward at the Solovievka.

A village girl who had tried to poison herself with vinegar essence told me that she had experienced a stupor similar to mine: she had put the bottle to her lips and fallen asleep till dawn. Then it was as if someone had given her a push and she managed to swallow it all before anyone in the house woke up. "I drank it down like water," she told me. This probably happens often. But no one gave me a push.

At the Solovievka I relived everything that had happened when I was on the mountain. This is why I say that will functions at a level deeper than consciousness. I do not know whether it was a dream or hallucination, but it is impossible to put into words. There I was, frozen for a second time on the viewing platform, when I stepped off it and landed on an unsteady, soft, yet firm, foothold like a wing. Beneath this wing, towns and seas slipped past. There's Paris, I observed. But it did not feel as if I were flying. I was being asked to consent to something (to what, I still do not know, whether good or bad), but I refused. And having refused, I found myself on the slope

161

once more and then suddenly in a bed surrounded by the utterly insane: one was prancing like a child shouting "Hurray, the war is over!" Another was walking around naked—in a word, they were lost in their own worlds.

"The world works by folly," said Baudelaire.[112] And I will gladly finish my tale about these personal circumstances. The sad end to this one (it could be worse) of course casts an even light of psychopathology over everything that precedes it. What can you do?

I would just note that a sick consciousness has its own reality. I recently saw a vivid illustration of this reality near the former monastery at Bakhchisarai.[113] Walking down the steps to the caves and coming up from them were tourists and tour guides talking, laughing, and enjoying themselves. But down below in the valley was a psychiatric clinic clearly visible from the steps. There in the grounds was a woman rocking an absent child, another was pacing like a commander before a decisive battle, a third was crawling on her knees and howling, hands raised up. All these actions lacked any object: there was no child being rocked, no battle to decide, no ghost to wail before. There was only the conviction and passion of the actions, the all-absorbing intensity of profound existence.

> Sein Wachstum ist: der Tiefbesiegte
> Von immer Größerem zu sein.[114]

A connection was being forged between the inconceivable sufferings of these possessed minds and the desecrated empty graves of the monks in the caves that we and the tourists saw: neither the sick of mind nor the monks had been able to live outside their own lives, beyond the most real question about the meaning that carried their lives along as a whirlwind carries a twig. We got along without this question, but many wanted to get along better still. They complained to the local authorities about why, "where people come for a holiday," this building was put here, why remind them about the "difficult things" of life. I fear that we are starting to consider a normal consciousness (not in science but in everyday life) to be the simple absence of human consciousness, the flow of acquired reflexes over a very limited scope of external circumstances. Many of these totally external circumstances are considered, at that, to be too slight or insignificant to react to, let alone any non-external ones. I have seen enough of the banalities of psychiatric illness and am not about to polish its romantic halo. Madness is awful, like a prison. But is tourism any less awful? And just as other great works have passed into the scope of children's reading, just as the magical fairytale and rain charm have gone over to children, so do many human tasks pass on into the domain of psychopathology and mania. Normal people discuss them, while the sick experience them. This would not matter, but what if one day only everyday chores are considered to be trouble-free. As it happens this is an old story, older than Hamlet. "But whosoever shall say, fool . . ."[115]

◆

I return now to poetry, to my apprenticeship. For a long time and with no success I imitated Mandelstam. If I were now to write a study about his thoroughly metaphorical lyric poetry, I would call it "The Condition of Mandelstam," after Valéry's essay on Mallarmé. "After reading him they found everything else naïve and crude" (Valéry). At one point during the sixties the same thing happened here with Mandelstam. Evidently his contemporaries did not set such store by him (see the articles on Mandelstam by Zhirmunsky, Tynianov, et al.). But a great deal was also thought to be naïve and crude. Even Blok. Mandelstam became the standard bearer for a philological worldview and "elitism." Everything about him came to be appreciated or became, rather, a benchmark: the fundamental verbal nature of his poems, the poetic quality of language; his ardor for structured composition; nothing "from the self," the pure crystalline emergence of form, the development of semantic motifs like *concetti*.[116] The impossibility of moral lessons and direct meanings. A tremendous indirectness regarding the immediate cause of an utterance and an elusiveness of the lyrical self. His "keyboard of references" fascinates scholars because the citations are, of course, also indirect.[117] An almost Pushkinian beauty, the calm air of sublime abstraction. There is an undeniable intelligence governing all this—an intelligence not only of judgment, which flees from the commonplace like fire, but also of the eye and of the ear. Even a nonsensical metaphor may originate, for example, from a sound that has been altered by many degrees (the metaphor of a metaphor). And how many things he has made poetic, as gifts to Russian poetry: stones, goldfinches, wax, all things dry, sharp; space, a link, a grasshopper; botanists and Buonarroti. All this has been clumsily assimilated, leaving the things that make Mandelstam alive unassimilated: the oscillation of meaning, the bare-wordedness that few hear behind his metaphors in the third degree. Moral lessons are impossible with Mandelstam not only because of the laws of "integrity" of his form (morals can deflate any form and we look for one in the saying: "You are eternity's hostage, held captive by time"[118]—and the pilot of the preceding lines vanishes entirely from memory.) Mandelstam's inspiration indeed primarily operates in this fifth element,[119] in the element of free culture, where there is no place for any ideology. Anything ideological and moralistic would seem here crudely prosaic and, possibly, insufficiently elemental and free. How will the weighty, clearly defined monoliths of Tolstoy, Dostoevsky, and other "masters" find a place in this "experience molded from the babble" of vacillating non-Euclidian meanings?[120] They will sink to the bottom of this art, leaving behind them "the wet mark of a saucer on the garden table," like Dostoevsky in Nabokov's novel,[121] or a "keyboard of references" with its flight of comparisons, like Dante in "Conversation about Dante." Their zeal for preaching is as inconceivable in this flickering consciousness as a linguistic barbarism, as bad style. It is with good reason that, in the "Conversation" dedicated to him, the "poet-theologian" appears to be someone else: he "lies fearlessly, plays pranks on Orlando, shudders, transforming completely,"[122] rather than achieving (according to a letter to Can Grande) "the purpose of the whole as well as the part: the removal of those living in this life from the state of misery."[123] And such a goal is usually attained not by jumping from junk boat to junk boat,[124] but with the fanatical single-mindedness of a pilgrim. It is no accident that Mandelstam omitted any clear reference to the apostle James in his translation of a sonnet by Petrarch: thus the double taste of water running from a spring became a metaphor for one of Mandelstam's favorite falteringly vague states, rather than for the assessment of a man's chances of salvation (as in the original sonnet).[125] It is with good reason that the "burning yarn" ("Night circles with a burning yarn"), which is an undeniably beautiful image, transforms the simple and traditional Petrarchan imagery (the chariot of the night) after the manner of Mallarmé. Inspiration, that departure "from space into a neglected garden of dimensions,"[126] is treasured most of all in Mandelstam's art (here he continues in his own manner where Pushkin left off). Everything that is ideological, moral, *ready-made* belongs in this space that must be left behind. It is this departure that he loves in his favorite old Italians, brushing aside the fact that they are not going out into a "neglected garden" but into domains ruled with lines, checking their course against maps drawn up by Aristotle, Augustine, Aquinas, and other travellers of those parts.

But, while taking my leave from Mandelstam, I am even more against his opponents: for example, the "supporters of Blok" (remember what Dmitri Maksimov would say: "The personal for Mandelstam was really always an 'Alexander Gertsovich,' whom he would attempt to recast within himself and in whose place he constructed an aesthetic personality.")[127] Valéry noted that there was something ethical in Mallarmé's exacting aestheticism. And there is also something ethical present in Mandelstam's "aesthetic personality": it is a sense of sobriety and conscientiousness, as opposed to an irresponsibly accentuated lyricism, a "carousing sincerity" (which for many amounts to poetic feelings) and feuilleton sentiments festooned with similes. This "aesthetic personality" is an achievement not only for Mandelstam, but for all poetry: it is a fine sounding-board resonating to everything around us, in the place of "self-expression." Whether this results from a poverty of personality or from overcoming a sense of one's own theatricality and—even more than theatricality—something that talks, interrupts, refuses to listen—who can say? Mandelstam reminds us, perhaps with an exaggerated urgency, of the chasteness of artistic meaning—of the author's subordination to laws of integrity concerning the work of art. He reminds us of what style, in the broader sense, is.

If the well-known expression "style is the man" is at all fair, then the contrary is at least equally fair, if not more so: "style is not the man" and "the man is not style" ("too broad, I'd have him narrower," as Karamazov says.)[128] In this failure of style to coincide with the man (indeed, a failure of "broader style" to coincide with "the man of his time," and of individual style to coincide with the author's personality in all its "excessive broadness," in all its stylistic polymorphism or amorphism) lies the fatal merit and fatal shortcoming of style. Style precedes personality, it is poorer, more direct—but also more fixed and certain. It forces Dante in the Latin eclogues to compare the composing of the songs in "Paradise" to the milking of goats. It forces everyone to do something. Where does its predominance over our sincerer impulses come from? Who knows. So what precisely does it force us to do with ourselves? Two things: first, to reject a great deal of our potential that we intuitively sense is inappropriate for the composition ahead (this is a potential of thought, feeling, theme, linguistic wealth, imagination and much more); second, to find (and not, I think, to create) in ourselves that potential which, despite excess "broadness," we lack in our conscious field of self-knowledge. The first thing is felt more powerfully and painfully; perhaps it is an impetus for a change of style. Counter to it rises a desire for simplicity and transparency of expression which, from the outside, are often seen as over-complication and overelaboration. The second demand coincides in many ways with a hazy conception of inspiration, illumination, insight: with the discovery within oneself of something transcending the self. You see, to speak more modestly, a perfect, flawless thing is impossible, but here's what is possible: the completion of a task that you personally, based on the sum of your past and present, are incapable of completing. This is possible and has been attested to numerous times. Let me remind you of the story of St. Francis and the golden spheres. Of course I mean the ideal instance of the relationship between Man and Style, which is unrecognizably distorted in many real cases.

We return now to the truth in Buffon's words "Style is the man," but in a sense contrary to widespread interpretation.[129] Style is not "man" as "he is," but man as he who limits and discovers himself, going beyond the bounds of his unique reality by means of narrowing and applying it to something taken as an external imperative and internal desire all at once. Style is also fostered by that inner addressee of speech, the Ideal Reader, from whose imagined desires and taste the crystal of style grows. It is with good reason that Mandelstam values the "reader, teacher, doctor" so highly.[130]

Mandelstam's "fifth element" today belongs to philologists from Taranovsky's school, and I doubt that anything new can be said in this language.[131] As for "one's own," "the personal," with Mandelstam, it seems to me that essential here is not his "now, now, it's all the same," but a kind of dalliance with the repugnant, monstrous, dangerous ("There's the smell of post office glue by the Moscow river"), an attempt to domesticate it, enchant it.[132] Even before he had real cause (as often happens with "one's own"), long before the "bubbles of air, culture and water" of Stalinist Moscow, this direction is evident in the Egyptian theme of his early poems.[133]

And besides, it is pointless trying to say anything in another's language, whatever that may be. I know the grim consequences of having other passions: such as for Tsvetaeva, Pasternak, members of the OBERIU[134] (who were imitated by half of Moscow and Leningrad; and it is strange to see how tiresomely predictable their absurd free associations, macaronic style, and breaks in meter can become), or for "difficult" foreign-language poets such as Dylan Thomas and Joseph Brodsky. Even the seemingly neutral later poetry of Akhmatova will not work to anyone's advantage. In a word, an apprenticeship blessed with fruits such as those of Statius under Virgil, as described by Dante:

Per te poeta fui, per te cristiano[135]

is a miracle, as is perfectly clear without my saying so. I would gladly talk of a miracle such as this, rather than the less than miraculous manifestations of epigonism, but unfortunately I know of no new examples. They say that the new Catholic poets are successfully following Dante's example, but this is almost the same as following the example set by Poetry itself. However, not following Poetry's example is even worse than taking Tsvetaeva or another imitable lyrical poet for Poetry itself (Pushkin is no longer more imitated than Trediakovsky: the cut-off point for epigonic "models" came some time around Blok). The latter pitfall (following a specific poet's example) bears the threat of personal failure, while the former (not following that of Poetry itself)—social catastrophe: the creation of a poetic tradition outside poetry, as happened in Russia. Compared to earthquakes, plague, and hunger, this, perhaps, is not the greatest of catastrophes—but believe Pushkin when he says:

> Woe to the country where slavery and flattery
> Alone may find favor by the throne,
> While the singer chosen by the heavens
> Is silent, fixing his gaze low.[136]

The air of a country where the ozone of inspiration does not fan freely is poisoned, its waters turn cloudy without the purifying flow of the Hippocrene, the men "are not worthy of a sweet woman's kiss."[137]

Am I too quick in equating poetry outside Poetry to "slavery and flattery"? I think not. The non-traditional poet is, as Eliot says, "unconscious where he ought to be conscious, and conscious where he ought to be unconscious." "Slavery and flattery" are also a part of this mixture. The inspired—that is, traditional—poet cannot, even if he wants to, take on the role of slave or flatterer: his consciousness and unconsciousness, well placed, like a singer's voice, will turn with equal aversion from hitting an unquestionably wrong note.

Apart from Dante, one other poet is almost analogous to Poetry itself: Rilke, "the physicist."[138] I have already written about his physics and will not repeat myself here.[139] O gentle reader, we are not judged for our desires—I would have liked to have been something of a "biologist."

Dante's world is unimaginable as a landscape. If it is possible to imagine lightning in the form of surroundings, then this would be similar to Dante. One would need to be like Argus and rapidly switch between varifocal optical mechanisms, so as to somehow catch a glimpse of this world, or even a part of it, where an eagle's eyebrow can turn out, under close inspection, to be Emperor Constantine. Aided by Beatrice and interlocutors and by means of various eye washes, Dante performs a miracle with the human optical apparatus. His eyes caused him to suffer, and at times his vision turned red: his eyes were seeing their own blood. And it is no accident that his Protectress, the heavenly oculist, Lucia, also presided over hope: these "virtù"—sight and hope—are truly related.[140]

Rilke's world is easy to imagine as a mountainous landscape with a small village or solitary castle like his Muzot. In any country wherever there are mountains it is always the same: its essence is not in the architecture of the edifices but in the scale of the human and that which is not human—only in mountains is this scale so patently austere. By the ocean's coast, too. And this scale is constant, unlike the vacillating scale of Dante (who has a habit that we find particularly loathsome after German parades and our own: that of arranging people into letters and numbers). Naturally this is an internal scale and internal landscape. The sky there does not differ from the mountains and the brickwork of walls, or water from stone, or up from down, and God is not separate from the longing for him, which forms the material of these strata, ridges, trees, portals, and human gestures . . .

There is a parable, I do not remember whose, about art in the time of its enchantment with objectivism. By the bed of a dying woman are her husband, a doctor, and an artist. Who sees the events more fully? The artist, who is completely uninvolved, then the doctor and then the loving husband, who, in fact, is unable to see anything. But, it is precisely the other way round. The one who sees things most fully is the one to whom the events are happening, whose mind they are altering. There is no one who can answer Job's question. To put the poet in the place of the person experiencing the event is what Rilke wanted. It sometimes seems that his speeches delivered by a suicide, statue, or madman are contrived, that they are rhetorical exercises in the vein of Ovid's "Heroides." They express themselves in an utterly sculpted manner. But more often it is not so, and they overwhelm us as extraordinary confessions. Why do we wish to see the author as real and ask him: were you really in the madman's place? Maybe for the sake of the word, for the sake of its being heard through to the end (like atheists from simple folk: Look, I'll say there's no God—will lightning strike me?). Or, on the contrary, for the love of reality itself, for the love of what reality is not: neither a burden, nor nonsense, nor the dross of inner life where all this lightning really does strike. As it happens, the actual event of creation is rich enough for its material to suffice for the "real" events of Phèdre, Hamlet . . .

And this task, one of the most central to Rilke's New Art—to give a voice to that which is silent—seems to me a sacred and utterly audacious act of humility performed by poetry. This task is new, like all common truths—just like the wordless world from which such truths do not differ to the extent that very few can understand them. Remember what Pasternak said in relation to Scriabin about the festival of common truths that float about in the air for centuries, aimlessly and to no avail, until someone catches them and at last makes use of them. And then it will be clear what a wealth of unexpected fruits, arriving seemingly from elsewhere, the "commonplace" is destined to bring us. And Dante showed us what it costs to pronounce at the end the "commonplace" "on Love which moves the sun and other heavenly bodies." And Rilke showed us how much spiritual toil and asceticism is required to realize that commonplace truth according to which only the as-yet-unsaid need be said. And he, who demanded from all artists and from himself a rejection of the most intimate feelings, including love, concluded his "Testament" with: "My life is a special kind of love and it is realized now. Just as the love of Saint George is the death of the dragon, the act."[141] I do not think this is an instance of imposture or deception.

*

Of course art is not a confession, good art often less so than the bad. Of course poetry has long since forgotten how to set forth doctrine—and what would be the use of formulating doctrine in the poetic language of the new era? (Who in their right mind would compare Pushkin's reformulation of Ephraim the Syrian's prayer to the actual prayer, or the countless rhymed versions of psalms to actual Psalms?)[142] Our poetry, alas, must above all say something *new*, and remain silent if in the confession or sermon of its author there is no such new thing. Of course "spiritual toilers" have long since ceased writing poems, and when they did write, these were different poems;[143] and of course writhing around Helicon are demons, of which vanity is not the worst, if the most obvious. And that "newness" acquires demonic power in Baudelaire's "The Journey." And it seems the shadow of a Faustian pact must linger over every virtuoso.

And—on top of all that—on the other hand, poetry is in no need of being defended before those who, limited of their own accord, have quickly learned to hate the world and everything that is of the world, but have not learned to make distinctions or to hate their own utterly worldly hate (which remains untransformed by love) for the worldly.[144]

Nevertheless, despite all these "of courses" I assure you that poetry is a gift, a gift blessed by heaven and earth, bearing witness, if not to the "life-giving Spirit" (He sends His witnesses to other vineyards), then to the "living soul." And no one who knows what it means to be alive will say that it is a paltry or useless gift. I mean here poetry as we have found it: poetry that is secular and individual, as a historian of literature would say; and which, moreover, is a late flower of that tradition, poetry that often prefers "only sound" to sense and in place of all its themes—the extra-thematic tension of the moment, in which something is embodied and understanding unfurls together with the words.[145] Not only do I love this poetry, but I do not love those who do not love it (we have returned to the old idea: "The man that hath no music in himself . . . Let no such man be trusted").[146] Those who take it at its word, speak of its duties, want everything from it, except poetry itself. They are like those who complained of the monotonous taste of manna and longed for Egyptian food. The delight or satiation that lyric poetry provides is monotonous in its essence, when compared to the variety, power and wealth of extra-poetic feelings. This is mainly the sensation of something being transformed: those same feelings, meanings, words, forms, and the human personality—of the one who made this lyrical composition and of the one who is listening to it. Even the most sorrowful lyrical feeling unfurls to the music of victory. I would place a monument to lyric poetry in the form of the Winged Victory of Samothrace or the "Victoria, Victoria" aria sung divinely by Zara Dolukhanova.[147]

How are we to understand the unique sensation that crowns, for example, a triumphant monologue on all-compassing doubt, the futility of life and other scathing things? What can the author of such a monologue be glad about? Does he not betray with this most sincere joy an insincerity of that content which he has so tried to elaborate, to render triumphant and unvanquished? I think he betrays something else: there are things more important than any content. And that there is *meaning*, not the meaning of something, but meaning in general, that is—freedom and victory. The real victory, of course, is not that which is equal to the sum total of effort applied. The real victory is miraculous: it does not conquer that which it was fighting but is a victory over a total enemy. Over the disastrous state of man, who, by nature, is incapable of fully expressing his deepest self and making it worth listening to; over the incurable longing of the part for the whole; over the seemingly insurmountable transience of the world which "alas, alas, Postumus, is slipping away," and over probably more still.[148] The most miraculous thing about the miraculous helper of such a victory is that there is not any place where he is not present, and it is a matter of pure chance if he appears in one thing rather than another: the choice arises from equally wonderful opportunities.[149] What is more: the "personality" of the author (the author of a successfully completed work), that personality which Valéry called "momentary," and which Pavel Florensky called "betrothing the truth," is also selected from among a multitude of possible "selves" that are equally wonderful, equally responsive.[150] And when the deep-self is fully expressed, something else is expressed too, something that has dressed this "self" in different clothes, the clothes of "whatever you like." Either the poet's subject has been substituted without his noticing it, or he has truly succeeded in expressing his "self" (and "express" here is the same as "comprehend"). And, as he discovers, in the depths of his "self" resides a not-self, something different, new. Any elements of a poem that do not intermingle with the medium of lyricism, the element of victory—of the other and the new—are, I believe, prosaisms. No matter whether the style is common or elevated. Thus there are very few completely poetic poems in the world, while there is, all in all, a bottomless pit of prosaic and anti-poetic poetry.

Very few combinations of words amount to poetry: sometimes just a line of poetry, sometimes two or three words. There are some gourmets who love to savor such lines, to seek out and reveal ever-new perfection and subtlety in them. I instinctively want to lower my eyes before such lines, to instantly forget and then recall them, no matter how often they appear, and not examine them, convincing myself and others of the boundless possibilities of this beauty. A beauty that is far from safe: it is truly salvific, and there is nothing more terrible than salvation. If anyone thinks this an exaggeration, let them seriously consider just what salvation means. There is no need to fantasize on this score, for everything has already been said.

A large part of what history and the theory of literature calls poetry does not in fact possess this forbiddingly salvific power. It belongs to the domain of boredom. In an activity with so many limitations, such as verbal composition, there is a high likelihood of something boring being produced. More often than not poets either say something they did not intend to say, but have uttered through a slackness of mind, imitativeness or in the hope of an "it may work" or a "how about this." Or they say precisely what they intended to say (where the urge is usually to say something utterly shallow and egoistical), and then it is not at all clear why, for the sake of this arbitrary and vain statement, the cumbersome, but speedy and steady ship of form has been built over the course of centuries. Both the former and latter are boring and lead nowhere. Anything that is not boring and leads somewhere does not "objectively" stand out from the general flow of "poetry"—and if it does, then as a more successful example of the same thing. This in fact is not the "same thing," but something that exists in spite of it. And, close now to the eternally other—the holiday amid poetic weekdays—one must lay aside all instruments of analysis, all euphony and metrics, traditions and reminiscences, lexicons, stylistics: all quantitative measures.

If there existed a theory of poetry that had, if only in part, an affinity to its subject, it would show that the path to the general is not via the typical, but via the unique; that there is no law of poetry to be discovered in a generalization of the similar, but in a deepening into—not that which is unlike anything else (there is no such thing)—but into that which at its source bears no relation either to similarities and repetitions or to dissimilarities and the rejection of repetitions. However, if such a theory were to emerge, it would have to share the fate of its subject, that is, become unverifiable and open to doubt. And this is no fate for theory and scholarship. The study of tropes and meters and other time-consuming research of this kind deals with something of which poetry itself is ashamed—something from which poetry averts its gaze, and which, as a rule, theorizing poets do not touch on. They try to explain something else, but in vain: no one listens to them; no one is listening even to the strange similarities in their "theories from within." In discursive accounts the questionable subject of poetry becomes unreliable once and for all, no more than caprice and fatuity.

The irony is that the "objective," "generalizing," typifying approach to natural phenomena does result in "favors extracted from nature": power stations, new breeds of cattle, etc.[151] No such favor results from a theory of tropes: no one has built, or will build, anything from these tropes except perhaps for an effective assemblage of parodies. Do not think that in place of these tropes I would have felicitous or infelicitous chance: I find the image of a brightly colored pack of faro cards least attractive of all.[152] There is nothing more agreeable than laws and regulations. For example, the fact that when you drop a cup it will always fall to the floor—and not flutter around the room or write ciphers in the air—never ceases to please me. Even if the cup smashes, its fall never fails to please me. Why? Because we are still at home. So as to appreciate such a privilege—being at home—one must, of course, have something for comparison. Without this, the utterly predictable fall of the cup elicits only boredom, which it does for many. Then these bored people take their revenge in art, where they force cups to fly about in spirals and to chirp. There is little sense in revenge of this kind. If, however, you look closely at the inevitable fall of the cup, you will find there a spiraling descent, a chirping or anything you like: if only because these things are no less homely, regulated by law and fate, too. How are we to distinguish between a cup that chirps to express the whim of a bored writer and one that chirps on account of its nature, on account of a law having been discovered? An objective theory of tropes will not tell us. It is a subjective distinction. This is the final touch; for now all we need do is sketch in a rough outline. An objective theory of poetry does not believe in the content of poetry, otherwise it would pay attention to this content's topmost layer: the announcement that meaning cannot have gradations, that if we are to talk of things such as the "approximate" and "specific," these two addends will never add up to meaning.

Grumbling about academic studies, as all poets do ("To honor Pushkin or not, / perhaps they would never know, / without their doctoral dissertations . . ."),[153] is outdated and unproductive. I had better return to non-academic praise. And to my favorite common truths. What things do we call poetic in the clichéd sense of the word? And in the not completely clichéd sense: why are some artists (Rembrandt, for example) and composers (Beethoven, for example) called poetic, while Bach and Cezanne are unlikely to be called poetic? There are semantic overtones in the equally ambiguous use of the words "picturesque," "musical," "poetic," when they are used to mean something like "beautiful." As have I noted, musical is what we call a certain inner preference for the interrelation between elements of the whole as opposed to their each having a connection to something external. In altogether simplified terms, the musical is something beautifully unknowable, with all its metamorphoses. The picturesque is barely conveyed content, immediately present, and in common terms: anything that does not simply present itself to the gaze, but vividly strikes the eye. When calling, for example, a landscape poetic, we sense in it a potential narrative, something going on that penetrates deep into things. And where there is an event, there is a hero. And so someone will appear and do something; something will happen to someone. Do you remember I promised to talk about the heroic nature of lyric poetry? In common terms, the poetic is understood as that which is melodramatic, and this is not without reason. I may well be mistaken, but it seems to me that a sense of poetic beauty, unlike the beauty of music or the plastic arts, suggests something that is connected in an unusual way to the problem of personality. (Gogol, sensitive to such beauty, rightly concluded about Pushkin's lyricism: "this is Russian man as he will be in two hundred years." The length of time and the patriotic epithet here are naïve, but the underlying meaning: "man as he will be" applies to all great lyric poets. Not in a hundred years, or in a thousand years, but as man from any epoch when we think of him in his future.) And evidently part of this problem is the almost involuntary process of discerning, distinguishing the hierarchical placement of everything that, up till now, has been seen only as inarticulate chaos—and the dazzling annihilation of all hierarchy in the face of a miracle.

In moments of sincerity permitted to him by the author, the hero of plays and prose becomes lyrical. But he does not, of course, become a lyric poet, insofar as he is unable to transcend the limits of his "character," even if this character is as restlessly free as Hamlet. The kind of personality I have in mind when considering lyric poetry bears a negative connection to character: through its audacity to not have a character. Forget about all the qualities that allow you to do this and that, or stop you from doing this or that. In the place of character, we find beauty and the maximum potential of any character to see it.

"Man is above listening to my words which burn me, but Purest Humanity—the Church—will not scorn even my most pitiful babbling."[154] But neither pure humanity alone, nor any person who is above listening to burning words, is above listening to the most pitiful artistic babbling: he has never heard the like of it! In "life" it is unseemly to judge these "words which burn me" according to how new or well formulated they might be. But artistic sincerity, unlike the simple kind, is historical: it takes account of everything that has been said up to now.

The great lyric poet is a miracle of human trustworthiness. He is sincere—and not boring, not obscene, deceitful, or false like any sincere person, any person in a condition of sincerity, can be. In his sincerity we see what, in another situation, we would find unmentionable, repugnant, or funny—and look on in admiration. At the same time, he, like Blok or Baudelaire, might not experience any noble or gracious feelings and can in no way be a moral example in any of his specific lyrical acts. What has he done with these "feelings," with these "thoughts"? Has he forced sympathy ("Ah, poor man!") or agreement ("I'm like that too") upon us? Of course not! "It's as if it *should* be that way, and it is good that it should be that way"—this decoding of lyrical empathy is more credible. In the world of lyric poetry, as in the world of dreams, there is nothing superfluous or indifferent; everything is permeated with the energy of meaning. It is in this that the poet's words differ from those "burning words."

And more: the lyric poet is mortal. It is as though he has died already, even if he is still alive. We fear for him. Where does our preconception about the early death of the poet come from? And not just early, but *significantly* early. Why does it seem that a whole choir will sing out in a full and final rendering over a young man who has drowned, was murdered, or taken by consumption? It comes from the fact that *here* all this cannot be at home and has no place to go to. Death is present in the very intonation of poetic language: *here* they only speak like that at the very end. The meaning of this beauty speaks of death insofar as there is no place for it here—but it also speaks of immortality because when it appears it turns our mortal "here" into a foreign land. And the choice of such a meaning transforms sincerity. It becomes as if double-voiced: because not just any kind of spontaneity is befitting when "I am held as if in a powerful hand over a black abyss."[155] This is the sincerity of the plaintiff and, at the same time, of the judge, of the patient and the doctor, and lastly, of the cruel romance and Boileau. The second element, the "critical" character of this confession, is the very clear, yet difficult to define, character of exacting meaning. The first, "pathetic," element is the character of the man searching for meaning.

But the strangest thing perhaps is not this sincerity's dual voice, because even with this duet, and even with the necessary homogeneity of these voices, the poetic work might not succeed. It is the third element: the voice that forgets itself (both "pitying" and "comforting" voices are aware of themselves), which is what creates the lyric poet. For how unpleasant he is when he does not forget himself (for example in lyrical diaries)!

Thus the sincerity of the lyric poet lies in his most sincere wish to cease being himself, and not in the trustworthy enactment of well-worn "spontaneous feelings." Let us remember once more "The Galoshes of Fortune." How difficult it was for the heroes in the tale to extricate themselves from their fulfilled wishes. And how that bureaucrat, whose wish it was to become a poet, ceased being one in the wink of an eye. After waking up as a poet and starting to recall (in that sense we have already discussed) everything, he wishes right there he was a bird—and becomes one thanks to his shoes.

No one suffers as much from the caprice of inspiration as the lyric poet. The artist, the prose writer will always find something to do. Only lyrical content is so uncontainable and unclaimable. Suddenly everything vanishes: all your "thoughts" and "feelings," all the skills and material that are described by objective theory. This material is, after all, fictitious, and more than half of it is woven from the same material as the emperor's new clothes. Immortal works consist mostly of centuries of trust invested in them, rather than of their material, which is generally semi-illusory.

> I turn to you with a demand to trust me
> And a request to love me.[156]

These words of the young Tsvetaeva are spoken by every immortal poem from within its words, every great canvas from within its shapes and composition. Believe me, there *is* something that cannot be disputed, that we can never prove and that cannot prove anything, for indeed that is all there is. *All the rest is poor and pitiful.*[157] It is the object that emerges together with an understanding of it, a change in our consciousness that occurs together with the appearance of this object.

But lyric material is in particular capable of only an intermittent existence: it exists only on condition that meaning of some kind should emanate from within, on condition that revealed within the poet's personality is that essential "momentary personality," whose entire purpose results in the direct appreciation of this meaning. Indeed all lyrical work is essentially momentary. Neither previous errors nor exasperated final touches made after the lightning has struck (i.e., filling in overlooked places or misheard phrases) allow the author to enjoy steady progress toward the goal, where the object—like a long, long corridor—leads on further and further, and every step along the way is wonderful. Such continuance of meaning must be the business of the painter or epic poet. While in our case it's: not right, not right, not right . . . then suddenly, it's all there! For lyric poetry is more utterance than speech. And, as with utterances, approximation has no positive attributes at all, not even that of being of sturdy quality like "average" music or being able to hold one's interest like an "average" novel. Anything in lyric poetry that is not a definitive achievement, a "masterpiece"—is unpleasant, uninteresting and unsound. There simply are no "average" lyric poems, not even "average" similes. For they, these "average" things have failed to perform their sole task—to cleanse their objects of the poor, heavy, thick layer of ashes. There is nothing the lyric poet can add from himself: he has no colors, or tones, just words, words, words.

From the artist possessing "his own world," we unconsciously always expect his greatest piece of work. In it, all of his life's breath, everything that he has breathed out, compresses into a point, or one can equally say: in it, this point of tension that resides *behind* or *under* all his minor works will eventually expand into the cloud of one major work of art—behind, under or apart from which nothing can torment or disturb.[158] Just as, for example, the Rembrandtian world contracts and expands in his "Return of the Prodigal Son." Here the artist's personality has bloomed, justifying the existence of a particular Rembrandtian world with the fact that it is now more than Rembrandtian. The root of personality (and the style that corresponds to it) lies in a certain sense of being condemned to one's self: to one's self and nothing else. There are as many opinions as there are people. Each such incomplete and subjective opinion about the world is full of offense and guilt. And at the limits of this insular offense and guilt, without which not even form would be possible, we find that form is entirely free, that isolated meaning has become unique (which is more than becoming general), that there can be no other opinion apart from this unique one. And consequently, the incompleteness is no longer pathetic in comparison to the indivisible whole: this whole has many objects and is entirely present in each of them. For the incompleteness and contingency of the speaker and of his language, an object is discovered which reveals itself only for him in this incompleteness: and at the same time it is entirely *whole*. (This is a confused re-telling of the simple promise about there being *many dwelling places*.)[159]

From the artist we *expect* to find his name and home in a master-piece, while we *demand* this from the lyric poet, and do not want to hear anything else from him. And neither probably does he, which is why he waits so jealously for his genius.

Where does poetry surprise us most? Where it refers to the smallest things, those most overshadowed by objects of primary importance—to the pouring of tea, for example (in a stanza from *Eugene Onegin*). "Can it really be there as well?" we ask in delight. A multitude of things that are traditionally revered in poetry share the same origins, *ex humili potens*:[160] a butterfly, a stream, a grasshopper, a dreary road, old clutter, a dried flower . . . From the point of view of a person who considers it natural to disregard such things, poetry is indulgent, tender: it pampers those objects that have not been pampered with a symbol. From an even coarser point of view, poetry is childish. But there is not a drop of indulgence here. The poet, when he really is a poet, knows that there are no things on earth that can be indulged; that there is no point giving hand-outs to the wealthy, for there is nothing you can give them; that he does not have a store, as such, of spare meanings which he can give out left and right; that he has nothing, and they have it all. The fate of butterflies and other poetic bagatelles differs in no way from richly symbolic things such as mirrors, roses—and from here it is not at all far to "ideas." They all, in equal measure, are call-signs of something other than themselves. But if there was no magic pipe playing for the poet over their buried treasure, he would never learn any of this, or rather, they, in his prosaic mind, would never learn of this—of their own riches. The condition of poetry is not indulgence or a rich imagination, but responsiveness. To respond to signs that no one has actually sent out, just as buried treasure sends none out. The treasure itself is this call-sign, whose invisible and inaudible waves echo in the resonant trills of the magic pipe. But in another sound, another fleece.[161] And this new fleece is the image.

I do not know how to say what an image is, but I can give an example of one:

> Like a candle the darkness gutters
> and gathers round faces never singed,
> preserved beneath white shrouds,
> and the folds of those inseparable hands
> lie like the folds of a mountain's ridge.[162]

There are many things that can be done better outside art than inside it: does not rhythm interfere with "saying the whole truth," and is not regular, or indeed any, meter unable to "touch the soul"? But there is one thing that cannot be done outside art, that thing is the image. The "ideal," ultimate, artistic image is close to that *thing* of which the theologian writes: "The meaningfulness of material things and the materiality of symbols can only be proved if one's starting point is the thing whose meaning is fully materialized or whose material is permeated with spirit."[163] And for the image, unlike sentiment or self-expression, the language of tightened rules is not too restrictive. On the contrary, it is spacious. The image finds itself at home here, where it need not be ashamed of its inner pathos or its disparity to the world . . . However poor my translation of Rilke, the image remains. It is not as attached to the material of a poem as is thought. It remains even in a literal translation.

I would like to say here that the actual material of a poem, however dear to me, is not so very attached to itself. This material, which I have already called fictitious, has two principles: the word and composition. They stand in a rather strange relationship, as I have noted.

I do not know about other types of composition involving sound and color, but in the composition of words, the relationship between the component parts and the whole is reversed. The word is not a brick to be used for the construction of intellectual edifices. On the contrary, everything in the poetic whole is constructed and organized, including all contrasts and repetitions, so as to serve the word. And not only to reveal a supreme word, one which has never before been spoken by the language in which the poem is written, but which emerges from the sum of all the organized words like a distinct yet real shape whose sound is almost familiar (such supreme words are diligently sought out by anagram enthusiasts). This supreme word, "other-word," is simply meaning. The composition serves each of its constituent words.

For in each such word, if you listen closely, you will hear that other-word, which can gather a great many other compositions around it. Even the word "empty," for example. Imagine what a composition this word can unfold into, to the point where it is no longer itself, where, like every word, it can become a window with a view—onto what? Onto the appearance of something else. If I like the view opening up over this something else—for example, at the end of the Russian word *iasnyi* (clear), then all the words in other languages with a similar view will seem wonderful to me, too, and their sound will delight me: *chiaro, durchsichtig.* And it is precisely this condition of the word—as when in "clear" it is possible to hear or guess at many living and dead words with a different, but equally pleasing, sound—that a good composition must serve.

Would it not then be easier to cease composing poems and instead intently repeat over and over one such word until you hear through to its depths? Of course this would be easier. But this would, in the first place, be a personal matter for each of us, and the charm of poetry, apart from anything else, lies in the fact that it is one of the few *not personal* (that is not private) matters left on earth. Second, the result would not be particularly wonderful. In verbal composition, it is not the straining of the semantic possibilities of the word, but, on the contrary, their liberation that bears witness to the selflessness of the author, among other things, and the great power that can render the poet, a most selfish being, selfless during the act of composition.

The pianist Vladimir Ivanovich Khvostin, my great friend and teacher, showed me that it is the same in music: he was certain that it was enough for him to hear, and to let the listener hear, *each* sound of the composition being performed—and all the problems of interpretation, of "decision" would fall away. On the last sound of each piece he would take a large, unimaginable, *fermata*—and the sound would live and transcend all sounds gone before and bring them back and promise their eternal return . . .

Everything I have written here is what I think about "ideal," ultimate, miraculous poetry, of which there is little in the world. But not about "pure" poetry, which lies beyond non-aesthetic themes and tasks. The "otherness" of lyrical language is most wonderful where it coincides with the "ordinary," where it seems to be absent, as if there were no iamb in the three words: "I loved you" (*ia vas liubil*).[164] But there is one here, more so than elsewhere. The iamb of language itself. Gifts and wonders are most miraculous when they coincide with "natural order":[165] when we finally see this order as a miracle and gift through and through, as a sign, as news and as meaning without end.

Azarovka, 1982

AN INTERVIEW
WITH OLGA SEDAKOVA

(January, 2012. Translated by Caroline Clark)

Your essay "In Praise of Poetry" begins with a story of how the essay itself originated. Did you write it with only this one addressee in mind or did you imagine it could reach a wider readership? If you were to write an "ars poetica" essay like this now, some twenty years later, what sorts of things would you do differently?

This all happened during the era of the samizdat. None of my poems had yet been published. And to write the story of how some unpublished poems had been written was a crazy endeavor, don't you think? But these poems already had a readership: they were being typed out at underground readings—in the basements and lofts where artists I knew had set up their workshops—and drew large audiences. What is more, these poems had their own critics and commentators. Vladimir Saitanov, a Pushkin specialist and critic of our uncensored poetry, had in fact asked me to put down the story of how I had first started writing poetry. Of course, there was no question of this text being published. Who was I writing for? In the first place for this "commissioner." And in the second . . .

In his wonderful study of children's babble (those first attempts at speech), Vladimir Bibikhin, our philosopher, describes an interesting moment: the child pulls himself up in his crib and starts to babble. And though he's looking at the empty space in front of him, it's clear he's addressing someone and trying his utmost to tell this "someone" something. Anyone who has had anything to do with infants has seen this kind of thing. But here Bibikhin asks a question: who is the child trying so hard to talk to? And he suggests the following: the owner of language. I think he's right. And so the vague image of the addressee, to whom poetic texts, as well as this prose account, is addressed, reminds me of this "owner of language." Or rather—the owner of poetry (or the owner of history: for some reason I've always wanted to talk with history). Sometime later—and only later—a real reader takes the place of this "owner." But I imagine this potential, future reader to be, first of all, like this owner of language. As I see things, he is able to comprehend everything and has no need of minor clarifications: he must be able to understand more than I do. Who would like to find themselves in this position? That is the question.

> It is not for us to conjecture
> how our word will be heard
> and we will find understanding,
> just as we find grace.
> —Fyodor Tiutchev

Of course I couldn't have imagined that this prose piece would be published in French and Italian. I don't think that at that time I had even met anyone from France or Italy.

It was my first attempt at prose. I had been making up poems since I was a child, but I had no idea about how to work with prose. Back then I had two conceptions about prose: something along the lines of Tolstoy's "Childhood" and something like "The Art of Poetry." In other words: a short tale or a long tract. Two incompatible things. And Vladimir Saitanov's request that I write the story of my first poems suddenly brought them together.

Both these conceptions touched on things that were difficult to convey. I wanted to touch on the preverbal perceptions of my early childhood, traces of which still shimmered in my memory—and the beginnings of language. I thought of an *ars poetica* because I had realized fairly early on that the state of poetry in the second half of the twentieth century needed greater consideration, and that the innovation—that new linguistic freedom and depth brought by both European and Russian moderns (Mandelstam, Khlebnikov, Rilke, Eliot, the French symbolists, all of whom I discuss in this essay)— had not yet been thought through. All these names and works were simply missing from the realm of Soviet culture. It was Brodsky who first brought to our poetry the themes and concerns of the moderns and that canon of poetry they resurrected (the metaphysical poets, John Donne, Russian poetry from before Pushkin). But my guide into that world was not Brodsky but Sergei Averinstev, our great philologist and hermeneutics scholar.

What connects these two themes—the modern and early child-hood—apart from their coming together in my mind? A departure from the everyday, sluggish experience of consciousness. Children have this gift—of seeing everything as it is, and it was sought after by the new art of the twentieth century. It sought a *speaking* language. As the French philosopher and translator of Holderlin François Fédier noted, human words are constantly at risk of ceasing to *speak*, and then sequences of words will simply flow *past utterances* like some indifferent element of "ready-made words," quotations that someone or no one uses. "Words, words, words," as Hamlet says. And poetic language, in particular, is at risk of ceasing to speak.

Readers of "In Praise of Poetry" will see how difficult it was for the narrator to reach any kind of intelligible formulation of what she had undertaken to think about. In it I am not explaining to others things that are already clear to me: I am working them out for myself—and for the first time. "In Praise of Poetry" ends with a memory of Vladimir Khvostin, my piano teacher, and "Tristan and Isolde" is dedicated to him.

You ask whether my point of view has changed over the years and whether I would now write my *ars poetica* differently. As regards those things written about in the essay, no. I couldn't say anything else about these things. Over the years the focus of my attention has shifted, and new concerns have arisen. I'm glad that I managed to write all this down before the veils of memory drew forever. Incidentally, in the essay there is mention of a way forward—beyond the bounds of the modern, into some other realm. The names of Dante and Pushkin (in other words, the classics), a memory about ancient folklore—as we see, this is what had already shone out to me as the promise of a new clarity and new simplicity. A simplicity that has passed through the school of the difficult and a clarity that is aware of the dramatic tension of the modern.

In "In Praise of Poetry," you write with great vividness of the way that your piano teacher also taught you so many things about humanistic inquiry more generally, and about ethical ways to live in the world. What role has music itself played in your life?

As I say in "In Praise of Poetry," I was not in the least bit a serious musician. Music touched me, like a kind of ancient language which seemed to be more "former" than verbal language. Like a kind of indisputable statement. Valentin Silvestrov, a wonderful composer and contemporary, puts it like this: "Music is the world singing about itself." In reality by no means do all musical compositions contain this "music," in the same way that not all poems contain poetry. Generally speaking, there are very few poems to be found in the ocean of poetic production.

There is another, more technical side to music. Structure and composition, a piece's integral imperative—this is what, as I realized during my school years, poets can learn from music (it's no coincidence that Eliot's "The Four Quartets," as the title tells us, has a musical structure). Soviet poetry was utterly at odds with this view. I felt the kind of poems that were used here were "illegitimate": stories or contemplations expressed in rhyme, which the author could continue for as long as he wanted. For me, the "whole" poem is always more important than its separate moments. And the meaning of this whole is ultimately like musical meaning. It can't be retold or reduced. And individual words in the poem change when torn away from their everyday or lexical image—precisely because they have been placed in relation to the whole. I quote once again Fédier: the poetic word "is animated by a certain curve in its movement." It acts like light in a painting, like a change in height (an interval) in a melody.

Incidentally, the plastic arts, which are very dear to me as well, also taught me attention to composition. Often the antecedent of a poem has been a work of plastic art—painting, sculpture (predominately, ancient).

A further consequence of my attention to music and the plastic arts is the habit of thinking in terms of genre. Even before I know the direct "contents" of a poem, I'll know its genre: elegy, scherzo, etc.

There are more musicians and artists among my friends than poets and writers. And as it happens, they have always been quicker to understand my poems than "people of the word," the literati and even philologists. As they aren't used to asking: "but what does it mean?"

"Tristan and Isolde" has seemed to some of your readers as one of your most mysterious texts defying simple interpretation or retelling. Can you tell us how you came to write a poem based on this myth, and how this poem took shape? Is the voice in the poem an example of that "crescendo" of which you talk about in "In Praise" where a "heightened intensity of sense, sound and structuring" is reached?

When I was at school my favorite book was "Tristan and Isolde" as retold by Joseph Bédier. A small old book bound in black, and a wonderful translation, but I don't remember whose. As with poems I learned its opening by heart:

> My lords, if you would hear a high tale of love and of death, here is that of Tristan and Queen Iseult; how to their full joy, but to their sorrow also, they loved each other, and how at last they died of that love together upon one day; she by him and he by her.
>
> (Translation by Hilaire Belloc)

My "Tristan" starts with Bédier's opening phrase. But by the time I composed it, I had also read the original, medieval version of

"Tristan." Wagner's "Tristan" clearly has no bearing on my view, if only to the contrary. The light, delicate sound of meaning was what I wanted, and not howling from the brass section, as with Wagner, not the yearning of passion. I looked at medieval tapestries, enamels and miniatures. I listened carefully to the rhythm of medieval poems. What did this all tell me? It spoke of a life that had the temperature of immortality, so to speak. It was a world of joy and suffering, of deadly life and life-giving death. As Fet puts it:

> Where the joy of suffering glimmers
> And the object of this thing is not passion alone.

The plot of "Tristan and Isolde" is one of those central plots (myths) from the history of mankind that give us entry to an ancient, primary depth and allow us to speak directly about things which are final: goodness, evil, holiness, sin, death, and life. Working with myths is one of the most important directions of twentieth-century art. And it is here that I offer my version of this work. It is not in any way a deconstruction of the myth, but rather a shift in the direction that the Christian Middle Ages had started to move it. My task as such is not to retell the plot. The whole poem is a series of prefaces and digressions from the plot: it is a tracing out of the air, so to speak, in which a plot left "in parentheses" takes place. The play of sound and rhythm is a most important part of the overall meaning. Russian poetry contained none of these rhythms; I made them up. And writing in these new, free rhythms brought me true happiness.

I don't think this principle of crescendo is present in "Tristan and Isolde." The narrator's voice is always close to that highest, most intense point. And steps back from it—in comic episodes—so as to draw a breath.

I'm not a commentator on my own work. Ksenia Golubovich has written a very interesting piece on this work in which she thinks over and sees a great deal.

"Old Songs," by comparison with "Tristan and Isolde," might strike read-ers as one of your most accessible pieces of writing. Is this really so? Or is that simplicity deceptive, and as an author you deal here with complexity on other level? Tell us how this poem grew from one, then to two, and finally to three notebooks? What determined its final shape? You have recorded this cycle and often read from it at your poetry readings. What about the poem do you enjoy reading?

Are the "Old Songs" simple? Maybe at first glance. As it happens, one of my first tasks here, as with "Tristan and Isolde" (and later "Chinese Journeys") was that search for a rhythm—a new or older one that had been forgotten about by poetry in the previous cen-tury. If for "Tristan" I sought models from among Western medi-eval rhythms, here I looked for Russian models that were also all but unknown to Russian poetry of modern times. This is the epic folk poem (I of course adapted it), the rhythm of "spiritual poems" (something along the lines of Russian spirituals). It is reminiscent of liturgical constructions as well as biblical rhythms (particularly like those found in the Book of Wisdom, Ecclesiastes)—which is no coincidence: the "spiritual poems" indeed grew from these sources.

As far as I know, only Pushkin has used this rhythm in "The Tale of the Fisherman and the Fish" and in his "Songs of the Western Slavs." And in "Old Songs" there are echoes of these works. One reader joked that they are like "The Tale of the Golden Fish" written from the Fish's point of view, rather than that of the Old Man and

Old Woman—Pushkin's protagonists. My lines are generally shorter than those of the folk poem or Pushkin's, and the basic rhythm is clearer, more "correct." Why am I talking so much about rhythm? Because rhythm is the narrator's stance, it is the first requirement for meaning to unfold: it is meaning's real life. The focus is perhaps on how the original tone—epic or gnomic—moves here toward the personal, lyrical. The Songs are spoken in the first person (even when this person is not expressly named), and not in the voice of any objective universal truth, as in "spiritual poems" or the Ecclesiastes.

Once started, I did not know how many there would be. The Second and Third Notebooks did not follow on directly from the First. The structure and order of motifs in each of the three notebooks is complex, but it is for the critic to work out how one follows on from the other. The overall movement clearly leads toward the prayer with which it all ends—a prayer for the dead.

In "Old Songs" there are a great many reminiscences and references. When the Israeli poet Hamutal Bar-Yosef translated them into Hebrew, a friend of mine, who is a biblical scholar and knows Hebrew, annotated these images and references for the poet and told me that she had not previously realized how many of them there were. From the New Testament, liturgical chants, the lives of the saints . . .

I like reading poems from the "Old Songs" because, more than many of my other poems, they are for the ear and for the sound. They're almost songs, recitatives. The thing that I like about them is the quality of the word. The most "neutral" words are used, no rare words, archaisms, no outward "folk" signs. But the simplest of words—thanks to the rhythmic conditions in which it occurs, a kind of atmosphere of pauses—sounds out in unexpected fullness. It is as if these words were written on top of a silence that is by far greater than the words. The silence is not empty—but like that of the sea, of the forest: the depths of memory.

Your essay contains a certain criticism of the modern way of thinking taught in schools, for example. And you speak of poetry as generally preserving the worldview of thoughts and images that have more to do with a child's world, or that of the soul, which your essay describes as objective and belonging to the outer world. In your poetry such a worldview is clearly present and it strikes the reader as both a realistic and surprising way of seeing things. What, in your opinion, are the modern mental habits that do not allow people to see what you see or are trying to show them?

I refer once again to Vladimir Bibikhin, who wrote somewhere that our civilization is breaking the backbone of childhood. One can imagine that, say, in an ancient society or even in a medieval one the difference between how a child sees the world and how an adult who has gone through a particular school sees it, was not so fatal. The adult added something (a great deal, at that) to what he had perceived as a child, while not completely throwing out those first perceptions, as we do. Because what we are taught is the "scientific worldview." There is nothing in a child's experience that can answer this. He sees rain and perceives it to be a separate, whole, maybe living thing, like in Pasternak's garden:

> It's terrible! It drips and listens to hear
> whether it's still alone in this world . . .
> (from "The Weeping Garden")

But he is told about the water cycle in nature, the chemical composition of water, etc. He is taught the laws of physics, chemistry, and others—and is weaned away from looking at the world with grateful wonder. There is no leaving the path that our civilization has long since taken, and I am by no means for limiting learning to the mythological view. That first way of seeing things is in fact not entirely rooted out. They just don't think about how to work with it, how not to forget it—and even deepen it somehow . . .

And another "crack of the backbone" when passing from childhood to school is language. Children speak in language, that is, they treat words as though they are the names of things, real things. Education teaches them to not speak in language, to not select the names of things, but to "use words," i.e., essentially to move on to a metalanguage. Knowledge of a word is filled with whatever knowledge of an object that "we" (enlightened humanity) possess at a given moment. Gone is the experience of the word as directly linked to a world that named it; this is lost.

Art has traditionally been the guardian of a different kind of knowledge that does not supplant that first kind, from childhood. Art has not only been the guardian of this knowledge, but the place where it lived and operated. And there is one other "storage location" and "setting": religion. Incidentally, no scientific discovery can be made without its author keeping a hold of that freedom from instilled stereotypes and without his marveling, as if for the first time, at what is happening.

The unusual and unexpected are for me the real and exact. This is not the work of fantasy, but a cast of the world, *mimesis*, the imitation of nature. As Goethe said:

What is most difficult of all? That which is held to be most simple: To see with one's own eyes that which is before everyone else's.

To see with one's own eyes (or differently, as Pasternak wrote: "to see as others think and to think as others see")—this, for me, is the artistic gift. A musician would probably correct me: "to hear with one's own ears." But I am predominately a visual person.

This interview will appear in a volume of translations, and translation is an activity that has clearly played an important role in your own life. How did you come to translate, and from so many different languages? What translations have you particularly enjoyed working on? Are there texts you still hope to translate?

When I was still at school, around fifteen, I attempted a translation. It was a ballad by Yeats. I was captivated by the beauty and music of this ballad—and I wanted to try and see whether something similar could be done in Russian. I've always translated things that I like very much (that's to say, I've never been a professional translator who translates whatever's required). Some poets (Elena Shvarts, for example) consider poetic translation to be an act of betrayal against their own muse. I like spending time with other muses. It's not that I've wanted to be "reincarnated" as the translated authors, "play their roles" in Russian—I've wanted to express my solidarity with what they're saying and allow their words and rhythms to speak. I've learned languages with the simple goal of reading poets in the original. Italian I learned for Dante, German for Rilke. I've enjoyed my time with each of the authors I've translated and I've probably learned a lot from them. In Russia we have a misfortune that arose during Soviet times: industrial translation, the manufacture of pros-thetic poems. They are often very skillful (here it's customary to produce a versified form of the original with rhyme and meter), yet the poem retains everything except for what's most important: its life, intention, gesture. The main thing after all is that the translator be as sure of everything he says as the author himself and also that he relates his language to poetry in the first place.

My plans for translation . . . I've always wanted to translate some-thing from ancient poetry, from my two favorite poets: Sappho and Horace. Maybe I will have to put this old plan into action.

To return to the question of music—are there contemporary poets whose works create a particular kind of music that you admire? How would you describe the range of sounds or melodies in contemporary Russian poetry? or in that of other languages, for that matter?

You know these famous words from "The Stone Guest" by Pushkin:

> From the pleasures of life
> Music yields to love alone,
> But love too is a melody.

Of course, the music of poetry is not in its phonetic make-up. This is rather the *music of meaning*. It's difficult to define what the music of meaning is, as opposed to meaning without music. There is a kind of rhythm of meaning, and a metrics of meaning, a certain semantic melody, a semantic harmony, which is greater than the sum of all the words in a poem—and no one knows what it is made up of. I do not think of poems lacking this "music" as poetry. Most of the poetic texts I've encountered over the past decade contain no poetry at all. This "music" need not necessarily be beautiful, rich or varied—but it absolutely must be there, otherwise this is not a poet. The last Russian poet who possessed the music that distinguishes a classic lyric poet—a graceful, delicate music—was, in my opinion, Arseny Tarkovsky. In the elegies of Leonid Aronzon there is the magical music of meaning, in the poems of Elena Shvarts sound rings out with clarity. But all these poets I've named have already left us. Most contemporary poetry writers I know have nothing that rings out, in this sense. Noise, chaos, clutter—this is what their writing leaves you with. Out of those European poets I've happened to encounter, I was most struck by the wonderful music present in the poems of the recently deceased Danish poet Inger Christensen and the chaste sound of Philippe Jaccottet.

"In Praise of Poetry" ends with the notation that it was written in Azarovka. Can you say a bit about Azarovka and the role it has played in your creative life?

Azarovka is a village in the Tula region, at a bend in the river Oka. It lies to the south of the central Russian line and is not at all far from places linked to Tolstoy, Yasnaya Polyana. And it's not far from Tarusa and Polenovo—those parts of Russian countryside most celebrated for their beauty, with pretty hills, fresh creeks, meadows and groves. I inherited a village house where my grandmother and aunt used to live. I go there every summer, and it's there (usually toward autumn) that I can write. While my aunt was still alive I didn't do anything in the garden or house, I wandered over the hills and through the meadows and read at night. And it was during those times that I wrote "In Praise of Poetry" and "Tristan." It was an area of preserved isolation.

Now that I've become the owner, I work in the garden, patch up the old house, etc. And the quiet and isolation are, alas, disappearing. Like everywhere in Russia, here too in protected areas, cottage developments are springing up with everything edging closer together and becoming more crowded. Only the hill and willows are the same, and when I look at them from my porch I get the same sense of satisfaction as if I had done something good or just made up some wonderful lines.

What aspects of your work do you imagine English-language readers finding similar to contemporary writing in English, and what will seem very different? In what ways do you see your work as participating in literary culture outside Russia?

I cannot of course imagine how a reader of English poetry would read my poems. I first saw this "other" world when I first read my poems before a European audience (1990, in Glasgow). After the realities of Soviet life this world seemed so peaceful, so trouble-free and reserved that I was sure I'd go out onto the stage and do something improper. It was as though I suddenly saw my own work through other eyes. Work that had emerged in a cruel and enslaving life that was as foreign to my audience as theirs was to me. It all suddenly seemed to be intolerably candid, almost a howl of the type that is not let out in polite society. I read, racked with a sense of shame and of my being thoroughly out of place. But the room responded with an ovation. Maybe it was simply because I had read my work by heart for a good length of time—and this impresses Europeans. Modern poets (of whom I've since met a lot) usually read from paper and do not themselves remember what they've written. It's the same in Russia now too. This tells us about a different kind of work with poems— indeed about a different task. For me poems must at any moment have that same permanence and absoluteness as with classical poetry. Entirely there, like a crystal. I don't understand why one would write other types of poems.

Answering the other question is easy: at various times, various English and American authors have meant a great deal to me. I'll name only those who revealed something to me and where the traces of that revelation can be found in my work. In poetry: Keats (the odes), Emily Dickinson, T.S. Eliot (poems and essays), Ezra Pound. Mother Goose Rhymes, the children's folk tales (on which, generally speaking, all Russian children's poetry is based). Laurence Sterne's prose (his narrative strategy was the model for my "Journeys") and James Joyce. The essays of G.K. Chesterton. There's nothing to say about Shakespeare: *Hamlet* is the experience of my whole life.

Could you elaborate on the writings and cultural roles of Sergei Averint-sev and Vladimir Bibikhin, and could you say a few words about what each of them has meant to contemporary Russian culture more broadly?

Sergei Averintsev, whom I call my teacher, is, I believe, still relatively unknown outside of Russia. To us he was of immeasurable importance. In regard to philology, general culture and even spirituality. With him, with his lectures, books, articles on Byzantium and classical Greece, on ancient Syrian literature and on the Bible, I believe we saw a new epoch in our cultural history commence. It's difficult for me to speak briefly about Averintsev: much of my work is dedicated to him—work in which I try to understand the innovation and originality of the cultural and hermeneutic method that he introduced. I consider the meetings and conversations I had with him over the course of many years to be a huge gift from fate.

Another gift is Vladimir Bibikhin, our philosopher, whose work has not yet been published in its entirety. Not even a tenth of what he wrote was published in his lifetime. But now, year after year, new books by him come out (thanks to the work of his widow)—and I am sure that ahead lies widespread recognition of his thought, both in Russia and throughout the world. A translator and interpreter of Heidegger and Wittgenstein, he is nonetheless a philosopher rather than a historian of philosophy. He had something of Socrates about him: he questioned the world and his interlocutor. He wanted to wake up his listener from the dark sleep into which everyday consciousness plunges us—and everything is seen differently and as though for the first time. The word and language were of the greatest interest to him.

I'm lucky that both of them, two most-unlike thinkers, were my teachers and guides, the first people I'd want to show every new piece of work to.

AN AFTERWORD
OLGA SEDAKOVA, ACCEPTANCE SPEECH, THE MASTERS TRANSLATION PRIZE, 2011

(Translated by Caroline Clark)

I was delighted and grateful to learn that the Masters Guild of Literary Translation has decided to honor me with this prestigious award. There is no recognition dearer than that of one's colleagues, masters of their trade. Thank you.

This prize has been awarded to me for the translation of poetry, and so I shall allow myself to say a few words about this dramatic and strange pursuit—the *translation* of poems. A thing that for many reasons is practically impossible: and yet is as ancient as European poetry itself. In any case, starting with the Roman authors (the Greeks made do without it) all poetic traditions have been washed by the sea of translations, transpositions, and imitations of foreign models. And emerging from this sea onto the dry land of the new language we have not only themes and genres but also rhythms and stanzaic forms—all skills acquired from working with sound and word.

The image of the sea and dry land came to me not for the metaphor, which is too simple for this occasion. It is not a verbal text that the translator of poems in fact *translates* (recreates); it is not a text made up of words that are organized by certain external, formal principles.

The majority of translators most likely translate precisely these kinds of texts. The words in a line, in a poem, are in fact different kinds of words. In them is not only the "dry land" of verbal meaning, but also the free element of the *rhythm* of meaning, the music of meaning, which is what makes poetry—poetry. François Fédier, the French philosopher, who translated twelve poems by Hölderlin over thirty years, came up with a wonderful definition for this not entirely linguistic nature of the poetic word. He says: "in the poetic word there is a *virage*, a turn." It is only in this way that the caesura can be stepped over. And the caesura is there to meet us at every step. Poetic speech, like musical speech, endures time, and, unlike everyday speech, it knows how dramatic time is, and how it can by no means be taken for granted that something will follow on from something else. Between each past and future there is this caesura, a kind of impossibility of continuance, which can be overcome only by taking a "turn" of this kind. The poetic word is not connected to the neighboring word, but to the whole. To the whole line, the whole poem—and, ultimately, to the whole of poetry as such. And I am not talking about a special, rare, or new word, but the simplest, such as "tree" or "light," which within Rilke's rhythm of meaning are one thing, and in Eliot's music of meaning are quite another. They appear in different places for everyone, taking different turns. And so it is in the faithfulness to this music of meaning that I see the poetry translator's task to lie. We will then hear not the "translated text," not an imitation, be it successful or not, but a living, open utterance—that which is called the author's voice.

I've always wanted to translate those poets (irrespective of the language in which they write, or the time in which they lived) whose experience of poetry's poetic nature was the tautest. These I love and I want to convey my love for them to Russian readers. I've wanted to *translate* poetry and not put it into my own words, observing the meter and rhyme (or lack thereof): that is, to allow the poetry to say what it has to say in Russian, and not replace its heightened language with something more familiar and conventional.

That, to put it very briefly, is my task as a translator.

ABOUT THE CONTRIBUTORS

ABOUT THE POET

Olga Sedakova (b. 1949) is one of the most respected poets writing in Russian today. She is highly regarded as a philologist and as a translator. Her academic training is in philology with a focus on ancient cultures. Her published books in Russian include *Gates, Windows, Archways* (1986), *Chinese Journey. Steles and Inscriptions. Old Songs* (1991); *Poems* (1994); *Poems; Prose*, two volumes (2001); *Journey of the Magi. Selected Works* (2002); *Two Journeys* (2005); *Music. Poems and Prose* (2006); *Everything, Right Now. Poems* (2009); and *An Apology for Reason* (2009). A four-volume set of her work in prose and poetry, including a generous selection of her translations, appeared in Moscow in December, 2010. Her work has been translated into English, French, Italian, Hebrew, Danish, Swedish, Greek, Serbian, Finnish, Chinese, and German, and she herself has translated poems by Eliot, Dickinson, Claudel, Celan, Pound, Mallarmé, Rilke, Ronsard, St. Francis, Petrarch, and Dante. Her many honors include the Andrei Belyi Prize (1983), the Paris Prize for a Russian Poet (1991), the Vladimir Solovyov Prize in the Vatican (1998), the Solzhenitsyn Prize (2003), the Premio Camposampiero (2010), the Dante Alighieri Prize (2011), and the Masters Translation Prize (2011). She teaches at Moscow State University in the

Department of World Literature, and at the Moscow Seminary. She has taught seminars on Dante and on Pushkin, and she has taught many Russian poets, including contemporary poets, at, among other places, Keele University, the University of Wisconsin-Madison, and Stanford University. She has read her poetry by invitation at many international festivals in the United States and across Europe.

ABOUT THE TRANSLATORS

Caroline Clark is a British poet and essayist, originally from South-east England. She was first published as a "chosen young poet" by *Agenda* in 2008 and featured in the 50th anniversary edition of *Agenda* in 2009 as a "voice from a new generation of poets." Her work has also appeared in *Poetry Review, PN Review,* and *The Malahat Review,* among other journals. She holds degrees from the Universities of Sussex and Exeter, and her dissertation was on the poetics of Osip Mandelstam and Paul Celan. She has recently returned to England after having lived in Moscow for eight years and Montreal for six. Her first book of poems, *Say Yes in Russian,* appeared from Agenda Editions (in the UK) in 2012.

Ksenia Golubovich is a Russian writer, philologist, editor, and translator living in Moscow. She graduated from the Faculty of Philology of Moscow State University, with a graduate degree in English Literature. She is an author of *Seven Poets, Four Days, One Book,* which appeared in English in 2009, and of many works of prose in Russian. An organizer of the *Dictionary of War* project, she is an editor at the Logos publishing house, known for its publications in philosophy, cultural theory, and literature. She has translated a range of writers, from Bruce Chatwin to Charles Sanders Pierce and Ezra Pound. Her books in Russian include *Personae: Poems in Prose* (2002); *Wishes Granted* (2005; long-listed for the Russian Booker Prize); and *Serbian Parables* (2003), as well as an annotated translation into Russian of William Butler Yeats's *A Vision* (2000). She has held a writer's residency at the Iowa International Writing Program, and writes for the *Novaya Gazeta* newspaper in Moscow.

Stephanie Sandler is an American scholar of Russian poetry and a translator of contemporary Russian poetry into English. Her books include *Distant Pleasures: Alexander Pushkin and the Writing of Exile* (1989) and *Commemorating Pushkin: Russia's Myth of a National Poet* (2004), as well as edited collections on Russian poetry, on sexuality and the body in Russian culture, and on ideas of the self in Russian history. Her work in progress includes a study of contemporary Russian poetry; an edited volume of scholarly essays about Olga Sedakova; and, with three other scholars, a *History of Russian Literature* for Oxford University Press. Among her previous translations of contemporary poets are works by Elena Shvarts and Elena Fanailova. Elena Fanailova's *The Russian Version*, done with Genya Turovskaya, won the 2010 Best Translated Book Award for poetry. She is Ernest E. Monrad Professor of Slavic Languages and Literatures at Harvard University.

ENDNOTES

1. Allen Grossman with Mark Halliday, *The Sighted Singer: Two Works on Poetry for Readers and Writers* (Baltimore, Md.: The Johns Hopkins University Press, 1992), p. ix.

2. Mikhail Gronas, *Cognitive Poetics and Cultural Memory: Russian Literary Mnemonics* (London: Routledge Press, 2011), p. 143, n. 2.

3. Three poems read in Russian from "Tristan and Isolde" (as well as one from "Old Songs") can be heard on the poet's author page at Litkarta: http://www.litkarta.ru/ russia/moscow/persons/sedakova-o/. The recordings available on CD as of this writing are *"Ty gori, nividimoe plamia": Poeticheskoe vecher v Arkhangel'ske*, recorded in 2003, released in 2005 by Obshchina Khrama Sreteniia Gospodnia, Arkhangel'sk; and the book and CD set *Dve knigi: Starye pesni, Tristan i Izol'da*. (St. Petersburg: Izd-vo Sergeia Khodova, 2008). The cycle "Old Songs" is on both these CDs as well, also in Russian.

4. See Sedakova, "Puteshestvie s zakrytymi glazami: Pis'ma o Rembrandte," *Kontinent*, no. 130 (2006).

5. Valentina Polukhina, "Conform Not to this Age: An Interview with Olga Sedakova," *Reconstructing the Canon: Russian Writing in the 1980s*, ed. Arnold McMillin (Amsterdam: Harwood Academic Publishers, 2000), p. 67.

6. "In Praise of Poetry" was published as a samizdat in 1982.

7. Quote from a poem by Baratynski: "My gift is scant and voice is weak." The "reader in posterity" is from the same poem: "And as I found a friend in my generation, / A reader in posterity I will find." 1828.

8. "Our First Poet"—that is to say, Pushkin.

9. The family moved to China for a brief period when the author's father, a military engineer with a career in the Red Army, was invited to the Chinese capital. Sedakova lived in Peking between the ages of one and two.

10. Vasily Trediakovsky, Russian linguist and poet (1703-1769); he advocated a reform of Russian versification with his New and Brief Method for Composing Russian Verse, 1735.

11. Elena Shvarts, 1948-2010, Russian poet born in Leningrad. A friend of the author and of V.A. Saitanov. The quotation is from "Several views of the stars (a lesser fugue)."

12. Alexander Pushkin (1799-1837), "I visited once more," 1835.

13. Anna Akhmatova (1889-1966), "Poem without a Hero," part 2, verse 13.

14. Terms used here are taken from syntactic theory concerning the actual division of the sentence. Every utterance is divided into the theme (that which is already known) and the rheme (the message being communicated). This division does not correspond to the grammatical units of the subject and predicate.

15. A reference to "Woe unto you, scribes and Pharisees, hypocrites! for ye are like unto whited sepulchres . . ." From the Gospel of Matthew 23:27-28.

16. A reference to Gogol as the author of *Selected Passages from Correspondence with Friends* (1847) rather than as the great author and writer of "The Government Inspector" (1836). Two personality traits are much noted in Gogol: that of the great artist and that of the moralist, a quality that emerged most clearly in his *Selected Passages*, where he attempts to openly preach Christian truths. To become another author of *Selected Passages* would mean to become a moralist without having first written the more famous play.

17. Leo Tolstoy described experiencing a terrible fear of death in a hotel in Arzamas.

18. This poem is written using the Latin alphabet with the exception of Cyrillic sibilants (ч, ш). A literal translation follows it.

19. Anton Delvig (1798-1831), "To Pushkin," 1815.

20. A song from the times of the civil war containing the lines: "So went the plucky squadrons of the Amur partisans."

21. Fyodor Glinka (1786-1880), "Moscow," 1840. The "thou" here is Moscow.

22. In the original Russian, the word *dyshít* (breathes) is stressed on the final syllable with an archaic stress. Such stresses were used by Russian poets in the eighteenth century. These poets came to be viewed as the founders of modern Russian poetry with their Europeanized syllabo-tonic system that was modeled on German poetry.

23. Ivan Krylov (1769-1844), creator of the Russian fable. Writing in verse, he initially based his fables on classical Greek and Latin traditions and that of the French (Aesop, Phaedrus, La Fontaine).

24. Nekrasov's first poems were weak imitations of Pushkin's style. He later found his own style, about which he wrote:

> No harmony runs through you freely,
> My labored, graceless verse!

And so began the democratic epoch of Russian poetry, replacing the aristocratic "golden age" of Pushkin.

25. Russian formalism was a school of literary theory and criticism that flourished in 1920s Moscow and Leningrad. Scholars such as Victor Shklovsky, Boris Eichenbaum, and Yuri Tynianov developed their new literary science to theorize that originality in literature was only possible by fighting automatism. Shklovsky's doctrines of "art as device" and of "estrangement" as a principle of literary discourse argued that the aim of art was to distort reality rather than represent it clearly. The artist does this by using a set of devices to make an original work of poetic language and counter any "automatism of perception." The formalists' scientific method was revived when it was introduced in the West in the 1960s by a second generation of Soviet linguists and literary critics who developed structuralist theories.

26. "The path from inwardness to greatness goes through sacrifice." The words of essayist Rudolf Kassner used by Rainer Maria Rilke (1875-1926) as the epigraph for his poem "Turning Point," 1914.

27. Viktor Aksyuchits (1949, Belorussia): at the time when "In Praise of Poetry" was being written Aksyuchits was a dissident and philosopher of religion in the spirit of the Nikolai Berdyaev, considering the positive aspects of the Fall. During perestroika he founded the Christian Democratic Party and become a member of the Duma. During Yeltsin's era he was active in the ranks of Russia's extreme right.

28. Boris Pasternak (1890-1960), *Safe Conduct*, 1930.

29. Alexander Blok (1880-1921), "To Pushkin House," 1921.

30. Pushkin, *Stone Guest*, 1830.

31. Blok, "The Stranger," 1906.

32. Leonid Aronzon (1939-1970) a poet from Leningrad, of Brodsky's generation. Apart from some children's poems, very little of his work was published during his lifetime. He was involved with the underground samizdat *Sirena* and had work published abroad. He died of a self-inflicted gunshot wound at the age of thirty in Tashkent. The quotation here is from his poem "Now it trembles, now not at all," 1970.

33. A poem by children's poet Korney Chukovsky (1882-1969). Children across Russia know this verse tale by heart. In it the dishes and utensils take offense at the slovenly housewife Fedora and run away. She regrets her ways and runs after the plates, irons, etc., and asks their forgiveness, promising to love, clean and look after them. They return and all ends with idyllic harmony between Fedora and her dishes.

34. Rilke, "Music," 1906: "Strong is your life, but your song is stronger."

35. Fyodor Tiutchev (1803-1873), "Poetry," 1850.

36. Pushkin, "The Hero," 1830.

37. Ibid.

38. Pushkin, "Egyptian Nights," 1835.

39. Tertullian, ecclesiastical writer, born circa 160 at Carthage: "The soul is by nature Christian."

40. Virgil's Fourth Eclogue, composed circa 42 B.C., is often called the "Messianic" eclogue in which the birth of a child heralds a new Golden Age. Christian scholars of the fourth and fifth centuries A.D. saw it as an instance of prophetic pagan writing. Virgil was considered to be a Christian poet for the most part of the Middle Ages, and it was for his renown as a *prophet*, signalling the advent of Christianity, that Dante chose him to be the guide through the afterworld in the *Divine Comedy*.

41. I.e., a type of art with strict canons, archaic or Medieval art.

42. Pasternak, "Night," 1956, "You are the hostage of eternity, / held captive by time."

43. Mikhail Matveevich Shvartsman (1926-1997): an artist of the counterculture, living during the Soviet period. He called his paintings "hieraturas," "signs of the invisible," and saw himself to be following in the tradition of Malevich and the Byzantine icon painters. The term "hieratic" comes from a quote of Shvartsman: hieratic art was a

revival of canonical art such as Medieval and Egyptian art, and of Byzantine icons in a new, non-figurative, form.

44. This comes from a Russian saying about the traditional terracotta or cast iron pot that could be placed into the flames inside a stove: "You can call me a pot but you won't get me in the fire" (Хоть горшком назови, да в печку не ставь), meaning "call me what you like, I won't do what you like."

45. Akhmatova, "Poem without a Hero." The "bauta" is a traditional Venetian mask. The town of Luga is close to St. Petersburg.

46. The "noisy streets" come from a poem by Pushkin: "I wander through noisy streets," which in turn is a re-wording of the Italian from a story about Dante taken from Boccaccio's famous biography.

47. The section discussed here reads:

> I, s otvrashcheniem chitaia zhizn' moiu,
> Ia trepeshchu, i proklinaiu,
> I gor'ko zhaluius', i gor'ko slezy l'iu—
> No strok pechal'nykh ne smyvaiu

> And when reading back my life,
> I tremble and curse with disgust,
> And bitterly lament, and bitter tears do run,
> But I do not wipe away the sad lines.

48. Akhmatova: "How could you, strong and free," 1922, and Osip Mandelstam (1891-1938): "10 January 1934."

49. In medieval Russian culture chronicles emerged as an original literary form and, starting with Pushkin, were greatly admired by later Russian writers. The chronicler was usually a monk telling stories from a biblical perspective, bearing witness before God to the truth of every event. This tradition remained a very important one for later and secular Russian literature.

50. Gavril Derzhavin (1743-1816), "The Waterfall," 1791-1794.

51. In Andersen's tale "The Naughty Boy," the boy is none other than Cupid, who, having been let in from the cold by the old man, shoots an arrow through his heart.

52. The background to an early, unpublished poem entitled "Danish Tale."

53. From an unpublished poem by the author: *"Разбей себя, как зеркало кривое, / перед которым встали — / и оно осталось пусто."*

54. The Russian language uses words borrowed from other languages to describe scenery/landscape: *peizash* (from the French "paysage") and countryside/terrain: *landshaft* (from the German "Landschaft"). The word *okrestnost'* suggested by the author here is not derived from a foreign word and has a Russian root.

55. The Holy Trinity-St. Sergius Lavra is the spiritual center of the Russian Orthodox Church. The monastery founded by St. Sergius of Radonezh and an ecclesiastical academy are located in the town of Sergiev Posad. In Soviet times the town was called Zagorsk after the revolutionary Vladimir Zagorsky. The city of Aleksandrov is located 40 km from Sergiev Posad and 110 km from Moscow; it is the industrial and cultural centre of the Vladimir Region.

56. The "Legends" were a cycle of poems about the Lives of the Saints. Saint Aleksei is one of the most popular saints in Russia. A number of popular "spiritual poems" are dedicated to him, including Sedakova's own "Seventh Legend" (in *The Wild Rose*); "The Return" (in "Old Songs," included in this volume) and "Sant Alessio. Roma," (in *The Beginning of a Book*). Mandelstam translated the epic poem about him from the old French.

57. A famous site where a truce between Moscow and Poland was signed in 1618.

58. Published in *Stikhi, Proza*, NFQ/2 Print, Moscow, 2001, vol. I. *Tristan and Isolde* refers to the cycle included in this volume, more fully described in the Introduction; the full title of *Stanzas* (1979-1980) is *Stanzas in the Manner of Alexander Pope*. It consists of four long poems, each dedicated to, or framed by, the work of a major cultural figure and addressing aesthetic and metaphysical concerns. Its coda is one of Sedakova's most frequently anthologized and cited poems. The poem "Fifth Stanzas," sub-titled *De Arte Poetica*, is in a similar mode and the best known of the group. It initiates a new cycle, *Iambs* (1984-1985).

59. The image of this house and the grandmother later became the origin of Sedakova's poem "Old Songs."

60. Among the texts composed in Azarovka are this very essay, as well as "Azarovka. A Suite of Landscapes," a part of the book *The Wild Rose: Legends and Fantasies* (1978).

61. Alexander Radishev was Russia's first revolutionary writer, the author of "A Journey from St. Petersburg to Moscow," a work for which he was exiled to Siberia. The sentimental aspect of this revolutionary work lies in the unexpected encounter of a

gentleman traveler with scenes of suffering amongst the populace: "I look around, and my soul is deeply wounded."

62. Pushkin, *Eugene Onegin*, Ch. 1, LV.

63. The poem referred to here is from Sedakova's very early work, as are nearly all the poems she explains in this essay. She also took the word for "wild rose" (*shipovnik*) as the title for a volume of poetry (*Dikii shipovnik: legendy i fantazii*, 1978). The word is tremendously evocative for Russian readers, associated as it is with a cycle of poems by Akhmatova, "The Wild Rose Blooms," (1946-64).

64. Tiutchev, "Poetry," 1850 (cf. footnote 35).

65. Tiutchev, "29 January 1837," written in memory of Pushkin.

66. "What nonsense, Tanya! In those other / ages we'd never heard of love" (*Eugene Onegin*, ch. 3, st. 18, tr. Charles Johnston, London: Penguin, 1979, p. 93).

67. Quotation is from *Eugene Onegin*, ch. 3, st. 24, again in Charles Johnston's translation, p. 96.

68. Frol Skobeev is a character from an anonymous seventeenth century tale, one of the first examples of secular Old Russian literature.

69. Peter and Fevronia are characters from a sixteenth century tale based on a Russian legend which Rimsky-Korsakov took as the theme for an opera.

70. Spiritual poetry was a particular folk genre, a lyric epos on themes from the Holy Scriptures and lives of the saints. *Dukhovnye stikhi* (spiritual poetry) expressed the real "folk faith" and "folk Christianity." Their favorite heroes were St. Aleksei, Joseph the all-comely (son of Jacob), and Prince Ioasaf. Grief over sins and a longing for paradise were the most favored themes. The distinct rhythm of the spiritual poems is at the heart of Sedakova's "Old Songs."

71. "Red heels" were the dandies from the end of the eighteenth century who would engage in "dangerous liaisons" and imitate French fashion.

72. Pushkin: "Egyptian Nights."

73. Pushkin: "There lived a poor knight on this earth" (1829).

74. Tiutchev: from his later cycle "The Last Love."

75. Faddei Bulgarin (1789-1859), a journalist writing at the time of Pushkin. He propagated tsarist policies in his journals; a severe critic of writers of the day, he was often at the center of various literary disputes. Pushkin wrote several satirical epigrams about him, changing his name to *Figlyarin* (which comes from the Russian word for "buffoon").

76. In Pushkin's "Egyptian Nights" Charsky is the poet-aristocrat of the tale and Pushkin's alter ego. "Far hence be souls profane!" is the epigraph to Pushkin's poem "The Poet and the Crowd," 1828, and comes from Virgil's *The Aeneid*, VI.

77. Sedakova has said that she has in mind Soviet Pushkinists who interpreted Pushkin as a Christian moralist; her example was Valentin Nepomniashchy.

78. Pushkin, "I visited once more," 1835.

79. Pushkin, "To a Kalmuck Girl," 1829.

80. Akhmatova, "Poem without a Hero," Part II, Verse XVI: "Tak i znai—obviniat v plagiate." "This much is sure: if they accuse me of plagiarism . . ." tr. Judith Hemschemeyer, *The Complete Poems of Anna Akhmatova*, 2 vols. Somerville, Ma.: Zephyr Press, 1990, vol. 2, p. 453.

81. Pushkin's characteristic means of forwarding the plot: something has not yet finished when something else starts. Something is still going on "when all of a sudden . . ."

82. Pushkin, "Autumn," 1833.

83. Pushkin, the words of Doña Anna in "The Stone Guest."

84. Mandelstam, "Octets," no.6, 1933.

85. Khlebnikov, "The sayings and sallies of spring," 1919. In recalling this poem Sedakova conflates two lines: "The little gold ball flies through the net / of a budding poplar's branches. / These days the golden coltsfoot moves / like a huddle of golden turtles." Tr. Paul Schmidt, *Selected Poems*, vol. 3, pp. 66-67.

86. Akhmatova: "And my heart lacked nothing, / When I drank down this burning heat . . . / The airy colossus of *Onegin*, / Stood over me like a cloud," 1962.

87. The eleven-meter high bronze statue on Moscow's Pushkin Square was designed by the sculptor Alexander Opekushin and erected in 1880. It has always been a popular meeting place for young people as well as for demonstrations. Pushkin stands in an elegant, lyrical pose: head bowed in contemplation, hat respectfully removed, as if before

a holy place. The statue in fact once stood before an ancient monastery, where there is now a cinema. In 1950 it was moved to the other side of the square and turned to face the other direction. It now stands with its back to the cinema, facing Tverskaya Street.

88. Pushkin, "I have built myself a monument," 1836, a poetic testament written after Horace's "Exegi monumentum," challenging Pushkin's poetic forefather Derzhavin. Like Horace, Derzhavin connected his immortality to that of the State (Rome and Russia, respectively): the poet would be praised "As long as the Russian tribe is honored by the Universe." For Pushkin the measure of his immortality was the continued existence of poets.

89. Ivan Bunin (1870-1953), "This short life's constant changing," 1917.

90. The Palace of Pioneers was a kind of youth centre where children could choose to go after school and participate in arts, crafts or science-based activities; future artists, doctors and scientists were able to develop their childhood talents here.

91. These were the young hopefuls of the 1960s. At this time poetry was very popular and some poets enjoyed the status of present-day pop stars. Evgeny Evtushenko (born 1933) was the most famous, then Andrei Voznesensky (1933-2010) and Bella Akhmadulina (1937-2010). Their poetry spoke of social themes and reality, following in the tradition of Mayakovsky and Nekrasov. They enjoyed worldwide fame, representing a freer and more independent voice of the Soviet Union, but in fact were part of the appointed literary establishment. The following generation identified with Joseph Brodsky (1940-1996), who was not a part of the establishment and was a truly independent voice, so much so that he was not, at the time, published in the Soviet Union. With him the era of the *samizdat* commenced, and in these conditions Sedakova's essay was circulated.

92. Acronym of "The Youngest Society of Geniuses," it also stood for *Bravery, Thought, Image, Depth*. SMOG was an independent literary movement formed in the second half of the '60s. It was the first to follow a long break: there had been no independent arts movements or manifestos since the 1920s. Up till the emergence of SMOG it had been a case of pure social realism for all. Its young members (17-18 years) were driven out of Moscow or placed in psychiatric hospitals around 1967. The most brilliant of them was Leonid Gubanov (1946-1983), "Moscow's Rimbaud." Sedakova dedicates her essay "The Lost Literary Generation" to him in *Stikhi, Proza*.

93. Rilke, "The last house of this village," 1901, from *The Book of Hours*. The lines in the text are translated from the Russian, rather than directly from the German.

94. A play by Leo Tolstoy.

95. From Shakespeare's "The Merchant of Venice."

96. Blok "To the Muse," 1912, from the "Terrible World" cycle.

97. Mann's *Doctor Faustus*, 1947, tells the story of German composer Adrian Lever-kühn, who strikes a new Faustian deal with the devil, and of the cultural collapse in the years leading up to the Second World War.

98. Vladimir Lapin (1945-2005): political dissident, a poet whose work was first published only in 1993.

99. Protagonists in Thomas Mann's *The Magic Mountain*.

100. Reference to Mozart's "The Magic Flute."

101. Approximate quote from Nietzsche: Deep is the night, deep is the night. / Still deeper than the day had thought.

102. The first quote: Mandelstam, "The Phaeton Driver," 1931; the second: from Mandelstam's "Voronezh Notebooks," 1931; the third: Pushkin, "A Feast in Time of Plague," 1830.

103. Paul Tillich (1886-1965), German-American protestant theologian and Christian existentialist philosopher. The notions of the "abyss" and "ground" are discussed in his *Theology of Culture*, 1959. Sedakova has translated another of his books: *The Courage to Be*, 1952, and written an essay about its importance.

104. Venedikt Erofeev (1938-1990), countercultural writer, author of a major work of the 1970s, *Moscow-Petushki* (translated into English as *Moscow to the End of the Line*). The lyrical account of a drunken man's journey from Moscow to Petushki by train, translated into many languages, it was first published in the Soviet Union in 1989. A friend of Sedakova, she dedicates an essay to him in *Stikhi, Proza*.

105. According to Tynianov's theory the poetic word is dynamic and bears two forces within it: that of "normal" syntactic connection, as in everyday speech; and that of rhythm, the "constructive factor" of poetry which unifies the whole and determines word choice.

106. From the Russian proverb: *a certain simplicity is worse than theft.*

107. The image of the "rosewater of Christianity" comes from the writings of Konstantin Leontiev (1831-1891), a Russian philosopher, who believed that traditional Russian Byzantism was the true Christianity: obscure and mystical.

108. Descriptive linguistics was deemed to be a "socially alien" area of research and prohibited together with many other areas of the natural sciences and humanities.

109. Voznesensky—see n. 91. In his youth Voznesensky was praised by Pasternak; he was the most original voice of the "youth wave." The citation is from "Introduction," 1961, which starts: Open up America / Eureka!

110. A lake located about 360 km northwest of Moscow.

111. In pagan Slavic folklore the One-Eyed Likho was the personification of Misfortune. Sedakova subsequently studied Slavic paganism. She wrote her dissertation and then a book *The Poetics of Rites* on the world of the dead in Slavic mythology.

112. From *Mon coeur mis à nu*, 1864.

113. Site of the famous residence of the Crimean Khan Giray, established in 1532. Legends about Giray inspired Pushkin to write his poem "The Fountain of Bakhchisarai," 1822. Not far from Bakhchisarai is an ancient cave monastery built into the rock face.

114. Rilke, "The Onlooker," 1901: "This is his growth: utter defeat / By ever greater things."

115. The citation is from the Gospel of Matthew, 5:22: "But I say unto you, that whosoever is angry with his brother without a cause shall be in danger of the judgment: and whosoever shall say to his brother, Raca, shall be in danger of the council: but whosoever shall say, Thou fool, shall be in danger of hell fire."

116. The Italian term "concetto" entered the Russian language to describe a technique that evolved in baroque poetry (G. Marino, L. Gongora): an elaborate conceit which becomes dominant, like a total metaphor.

117. The expression "keyboard of references" comes from Mandelstam's essay "Conversation about Dante," 1933.

118. Pasternak, "The Night," 1956.

119. Reference to Mandelstam's poem "The Admiralty," 1914.

120. Mandelstam, "Octets," no.9.

121. Nabokov, *The Gift*, 1937: "In *The Brothers Karamazov* there's the round mark left by a wet glass on the garden table."

122. Mandelstam, "Ariosto," 1933.

123. From Dante's "Epistles."

124. Mandelstam thus describes the Dantean flow of exposition in "Conversation about Dante."

125. Petrarch, Sonnet CLXIV. In Petrarch's poem the image of the double stream of water represents spiritual doubt and also recalls an image from James, 3, 11: "Doth a fountain send forth at the same place sweet water and bitter?" Mandelstam translated the sonnet in December 1933.

126. Mandelstam, "Octets" no.11.

127. Dmitri Maksimov (1904-1987), literary scholar from Leningrad, specialist of Tsarskoe Selo culture and poets of the Silver Age such as Akhmatova, Bely and in particular Blok. He taught at Leningrad University where he met talented poets of the "second culture": Elena Shvarts, Viktor Krivulin, Sergei Stratanovsky. He found Mandelstam's poetics completely foreign. He wrote poetry in the spirit of the OBERIU (see n. 148 below). "There once lived Alexander Gertsovich" is a poem by Mandelstam from 1931 in which he sympathetically portrays a man dedicated entirely to music.

128. Dmitri Karamazov in the chapter "The Confession of a Passionate Heart."

129. Georges-Louis Leclerc, Comte de Buffon (1707-1788), French naturalist, mathematician, biologist, cosmologist and author. The citation *"Le style c'est l'homme même"* is from his "Discourse on Style" delivered before the Académie Française in 1753.

130. Mandelstam, "Where can I disappear to this January," 1937, in *The Voronezh Notebooks*. He discussed the ideal reader in most depth in his essays on poetry, e.g. "About an Interlocutor."

131. The "fifth element" for Mandelstam is the element of culture. Kiril Taranovsky (1911-1993), professor of Slavic languages at Harvard, was the founder of a school of intertextual studies focused on Mandelstam's poetry.

132. "Now, now, it's all the same" are words spoken by the character in Mandelstam's poem "There once lived Alexander Gertsovich" (see n. 127 above), a man who lives solely for the "fifth element." The line "It smells of post office glue by the Moscow river" is from his poem "Where bathhouses, cotton mills," 1932.

133. This line is also from "Where bathhouses, cotton mills"; the original reads: "crests of repose, culture and water."

134. OBERIU: the Union for Real Art. The union was founded in Leningrad between 1927 and 1930, its direction can be described as post-avant-garde, metaphysical absurd. Work of its members (Daniil Kharms, Alexander Vvedensky, Konstantin Vaginov) was circulated unofficially in samizdat form. By the 70s their poetics had a great influence on unofficial poetry.

135. "Through you I became a poet, through you a Christian," Dante, *Purgatory*, 22.73.

136. Pushkin, "To Friends," 1828.

137. Pushkin, "I am familiar with battle,"1820.

138. Just as Dante can be called a "geometrician," Rilke, the poet of the "nature of things," can be called a "physicist."

139. See Sedakova's essay "On Rilke's Lyric Poetry," in *Stikhi, Proza*, vol. II.

140. Virtù, from the Latin virtus: feature, quality, strength.

141. Rilke, "The Testament." The translation from Rilke here reflects the Russian translation by Sedakova.

142. Saint Ephraim the Syrian (ca. 306-373), theologian and writer of hymns and poems. His hymns and prayers were very popular in the Russian Orthodox Church, in particular his Lenten Prayer "O Lord and Master of my life," Pushkin's favorite, which he rewrote as "Hermit Fathers and Immaculate Women."

143. In his poem "The Wanderer," 1835, Pushkin calls ascetics and monks "spiritual toilers."

144. This is directed toward Orthodox neophytes: recent converts to Russian Orthodoxy who deny or detest any kind of secular or worldly culture, especially a certain artistic creativity which they consider to be inspired solely by the devil. These new converts are as anti-secular as the Soviet atheists were anti-religious during the twentieth century.

145. "Only sound," reference to Trediakovsky, see n. 10.

146. See n. 95.

147. Zara Dolukhanova (1918-2007), a highly-regarded chamber and mezzo-soprano opera singer. She was particularly notable for her interpretation of Italian and German music, which was rare for the repertoire of a Soviet vocalist. Her accompanist in later

years was Vladimir Khvostin (mentioned at the end of this essay), with whom she made a number of now classic recordings. She and Sedakova were friends.

148. Horace, Ode 2. 14.

149. The idea of the miraculous or magical helper comes from Vladimir Propp's theory of fairy tales, as described in his *Morphology of the Folk Tale*, 1928. In the plot of a fairy tale there is always a "magical helper" who helps the hero overcome seemingly insurmountable difficulties.

150. Pavel Florensky (1882-1937), Russian Orthodox theologian and priest. His main work is *The Pillar and Ground of the Truth: an Essay in Orthodox Theodicy in Twelve Letters*, pub. 1924.

151. The widely popularized phrase of Soviet botanist Vladimir Michurin which people knew by heart from an early age: We cannot wait for favors from nature. To extract them ourselves—that is our task!

152. Pushkin, *Eugene Onegin*: "before his eyes, imagination / brings out its faro pack, and deals." Ch. 8, verse 37, Charles Johnston's translation, p. 226. Faro is a card game, popular in Pushkin's era, used in gambling and based on pure chance.

153. Pasternak, "The Wind," 1956, subtitled "Four Fragments on Blok."

154. Florensky, *Sobranie sochinenii. Filosofija kul'ta (Opyt pravoslavnoi antropoditisei)*, *Collected Essays. Philosophy of a Cult (Essay of an Orthodox Anthropodicy)*, ed. Hegumen Andronik (Trubachev), Mysl', 2004.

155. Anafasy Fet (1820-1892), "On a haystack this southern night," 1857.

156. Marina Tsvetaeva (1892-1941), "How many have fallen into this abyss," 1913.

157. A line from Sedakova's poem "Tale."

158. A reference to the line "nothing can / Torment or disturb my melancholy," from Pushkin's poem "In the hills of Georgia," 1829.

159. The Gospel of John 14:2 "In my father's house there are many dwelling places."

160. Horace, Ode 3.30, "from lowly beginnings come the powerful."

161. "With another voice now, and other fleece," Dante, *Paradiso*, XXV, 1–9, he dreams of returning to Florence, to the Baptistery of San Giovanni, where he was baptized.

162. Rilke, *"Weisst du von jenen Heiligen, mein Herr,"* The Book of Hours, 1901. The translation here reflects Sedakova's translation into Russian.

163. Florensky.

164. Pushkin, "I loved you," 1829.

165. "Where God wills, natural order is conquered," a liturgical hymn from the "Great Penitential Canon," by Andrei Kritsky, read at the start of Lent.

Open Letter—the University of Rochester's nonprofit, literary translation press—is one of only a handful of publishing houses dedicated to increasing access to world literature for English readers. Publishing ten titles in translation each year, Open Letter searches for works that are extraordinary and influential, works that we hope will become the classics of tomorrow.

Making world literature available in English is crucial to opening our cultural borders, and its availability plays a vital role in maintaining a healthy and vibrant book culture. Open Letter strives to cultivate an audience for these works by helping readers discover imaginative, stunning works of fiction and poetry, and by creating a constellation of international writing that is engaging, stimulating, and enduring.

Current and forthcoming titles from Open Letter include works from Argentina, Bulgaria, China, France, Greece, Iceland, Latvia, Poland, South Africa, and many other countries.

www.openletterbooks.org